NEW CAREER OPPORTUNITIES IN THE PARALEGAL PROFESSION

NEW CAREER OPPORTUNITIES
IN THE
PARALEGAL PROFESSION

RACHEL LANE BERKEY

ARCO PUBLISHING, INC.
NEW YORK

Published by Arco Publishing, Inc.
215 Park Avenue South, New York, N.Y. 10003

Copyright © 1983 by Arco Publishing, Inc.

Library of Congress Cataloging in Publication Data

Berkey, Rachel Lane.
    New career opportunities in the paralegal profession.

    Includes index. 84-641
    1. Legal assistants—United States.   I. Title.
KF320.L4B47   1983   340′.023′73   82–13929
ISBN 0–668–05478–6 (Reference Text)
ISBN 0–668–05482–4 (Paper Edition)

Printed in the United States of America

FOR DAVID

Contents

Preface

The paralegal profession is a unique one because it can be entered at any age, can serve as a career for some, or can be used to attain skills for use in other professions.

There are many people working in paralegal jobs who do not have the job title "paralegal." The word "paralegal" serves as a description of a job function as well as being a job title. Paralegals are involved in many facets of law-related activities, and work in law firms, businesses, government, and public interest organizations.

It is my hope that people wishing to become paralegals, those already working as paralegals, as well as lawyers interested in hiring paralegals, will gain insight from this book as to what a paralegal is and can do for the legal profession.

Acknowledgments

Many people deserve to be thanked for the assistance they provided to me as I was writing this book: David Berkey for his continued support and advice, Geri Barbieri for her excellent typing skills and patience, and Peter Michelli for his descriptive photographs.

For my own thorough paralegal education I wish to thank the Adelphi University Lawyer's Assistant Program.

For their insights and time, I would like to thank Mitchell Berkey, Carol Brier, Marion DeMuro, Carolyn Gaines, Ann Krawet, Nancy Lentner, Penelope Morgan, Rose Morgan, Vicki Schott, Nena Shanks, and Christopher Sullivan.

Special thanks go to Mercy College's 1982 Spring Day Paralegal class, its paralegal faculty, administrators, and librarians, for providing me with an on-site location for photographs.

1. Introduction to the Paralegal Profession

General Background

Since the late sixties, the legal community has seen the growth of a new professional within its midst—the paralegal. The paralegal, also referred to as a legal assistant or a lawyer's assistant, is a specially trained individual who works alongside a lawyer in virtually all aspects of the practice of law. Since the paralegal profession is such a new and growing field, there are questions concerning where a paralegal fits in within the framework of a law office or a legal department.

A paralegal is not a lawyer although he/she spends much of his/her time performing many of the same tasks as a lawyer. A paralegal is also not a legal secretary, although in some smaller offices he/she may be required to type his/her own work.

Paralegalism is a profession separate from that of an attorney or a legal secretary. Some legal secretaries become paralegals, just as some paralegals may go on to law school and become lawyers. Paralegals are trained legal personnel not admitted to a bar who must work under the direction and supervision of a lawyer. Although the paralegal is always supervised by an attorney, cannot give legal advice to clients, or represent himself/herself as an attorney, he/she is very much a part of the legal team.

Lawyers have always used some type of support personnel. The first assistants to lawyers, not including those training to become lawyers and scribes, were legal secretaries. As the legal secretary began to perform tasks in the law office beyond the scope of secretarial duties, such as legal research, drafting papers, analyzing facts, and summarizing data, the concept of the paralegal, someone to assist the attorney, crystallized.

The use of paralegals enabled lawyers to improve the delivery of legal services to their clients, and the cost of the lawyer's services was a major factor in this development. An attorney's time is billed out on an hourly rate or a fraction thereof. A paralegal's time is billed out in a similar fashion, but at a much lower rate, resulting in a savings for the client.

Operating expenses and overhead also affect the cost of legal services. The Connecticut Bar Association, in their pamphlet entitled *Lawyers and Legal Fees*, indicates that the cost of operating the average law office—including such items as rent, equipment, law library, supplies, professional and nonprofessional staff, insurance, and the like—is from 36 to 55 percent of the gross annual income derived from legal fees.

Fees and expenses can be kept down by the use of legal assistants. The lawyer's expert skills in legal reasoning and theory can be directed to assisting the client, while the more routine activities can be delegated to the paralegal. This works to the advantage of both lawyer and client, since it frees the attorney to service more clients, thereby increasing the size of his/her practice, and saves the clients money.

A properly trained paralegal can assist the lawyer in many tasks that a legal secretary simply has no time for. Since the paralegal is trained to perform procedural tasks he/she can almost immediately be given routine legal assignments which were in the past reserved for highly paid recent graduates of law schools.

Under the supervision of an attorney, a paralegal can draft briefs, cite-check, digest depositions, and shepardize cases (determining whether a case is still valid authority for the proposition for which the case is cited). A paralegal can act as a law librarian, keeping and monitoring legal volumes, and making sure that they are up to date. A paralegal trained in using computerized research tools can assist the attorneys with legal research. Paralegals can assist at real estate closings, and on occasion perform simple closings. A paralegal can draft closing statements, supervise the preparation of real estate documents, and monitor the costs relating to a closing.

A paralegal can assist in the preparation of legal documents used in real estate planning. A paralegal can help administer estates, draft wills and trusts, complete federal and state tax returns, and maintain estate and trust records.

A paralegal can help prepare initial and amended articles of incorporation, stock certificates, and other securities, buy–sell agreements, closing papers, and binders.

A paralegal can help draft pension and profit-sharing plans, summary plan descriptions, and prepare and file annual reports.

A paralegal can help prepare petitions, complaints, and other court-related forms, act as an arbitrator, and act as a liaison between disputing parties.

A paralegal can be used as an office manager and administrator in law offices. In reporting directly to the managing partners of the firm, he/she can set office policies, prepare budgets and reports, hire nonlegal personnel, supervise secretaries and non-lawyers, and supervise the installation of office equipment.

The United States Bureau of Labor Statistics has forecast that the number of paralegal jobs will grow by 132–166 percent by 1990. The kinds of jobs available will vary with the type of law being practiced, the size of the firm, and a paralegal's prior work experience.

Paralegals are employed in large and small law firms, legal departments of corporations, insurance companies, pension consulting firms, banks, consulting firms, government, courthouses, legal aid societies, and legal corporations. And new opportunities are continually opening for paralegals in industry as companies learn how this new profession can be of assistance to them. It is estimated that there are today close to 100,000 paralegals.

Initially the paralegal was trained in-house, that is, directly by the lawyer. This proved to be too time-consuming for the lawyer and also failed to provide the paralegal with thorough training, so eventually paralegal training institutions were founded.

There are several different types of paralegal training facilities available. In Chapter 2 there are descriptions of the types of training programs offered, sample curricula, and educational requirements for entrance into such programs.

Questions Most Frequently Asked about a Paralegal Career

I am a high school senior who is considering law as a career. Do I have a better chance of getting into law school if I get a bachelor's degree in paralegal studies?

Being accepted by a law school is contingent on several factors: undergraduate grade point average, law board scores, and, when applicable, an interview at the law school. It is usually not

A paralegal frequently works independently on assignments.

dependent on a particular undergraduate major. Taking paralegal courses while in college will familiarize you with certain legal concepts and principles, but it will not weigh in a law school's decision regarding your application.

One advantage to getting a bachelor's degree in paralegal studies, however, is that when you graduate you will have a marketable skill as a legal assistant. You may want to take some time off between college and law school, and by working as a paralegal you will get some exposure to working in a legal setting. And, of course, you will make money at the same time!

Should I take a generalist or a specialist paralegal program?

There are advantages to taking either one of these kinds of programs. With a generalist background you will study several areas of law and prepare yourself to work at a general practice firm or in a position which requires you to work in a number of different areas of law. You also may find that by becoming a generalist you have more flexibility in seeking employment. If you live in an area of the country where there are many general practice law firms and sole practitioners, you will find that by attaining an overview of several areas of law, your paralegal skills will be more marketable.

If you should choose to specialize in one area of law (this type of study is found in certificate programs), you will be prepared for a job in a large law practice where the work is departmentalized. By becoming an "expert" in one area of law, you will find that your employment opportunities will increase when you seek a position in a corporate law firm or in a major corporation.

I am taking a paralegal program in one state but will be moving to another state when I graduate. Will I be able to get a job?

Since there is no certifying examination or state bar examination for paralegals, there should be no problem. As you will find out, legal research will become a very valuable part of your training program. Do emphasize this in your job interviews, since the ability to use a law library is the key to learning another state's laws.

I am a teacher who is considering a career change. Would a paralegal training program assist me in leaving the teaching field?

Many people are attracted to the paralegal career when seeking a career change. Some paralegal jobs require excellent research skills, others require facility in speaking, writing, and working well with people. Since there are so many different kinds of paralegal positions open, you will find that people with a variety of educational and work backgrounds study to become paralegals.

A paralegal training program would give you a new skill in a relatively short period of time. With at least a college degree, you should choose a certificate program which would train you in the shortest period of time. Some teachers who have the summers off can take a concentrated paralegal program over the summer. They can then look for a job as a legal assistant in the fall. An evening program taking a year or less to complete would allow you to continue working while you study for a new career.

What is the tuition at paralegal schools?

The cost of attending a paralegal program varies from school to school. It may also be dependent on the type of program offering the paralegal training, that is certificate, diploma, credit, or noncredit.

The tuition at a state college or community college will usually be lower than at a private college. Proprietary institutions will generally charge the highest tuition.

Students in undergraduate paralegal studies programs may be eligible for federal and state financial aid. Students in graduate level programs may only be eligible for state education loans.

I graduated from college but never worked. After raising a family I want to enter the job market. Would taking a paralegal program assist me in finding a job either in the legal or some other field?

Paralegal programs are popular with women who wish to enter or reenter the job market but have no marketable skills. Of course, paralegal training is just one type of career that a woman can consider, but it is a profession which has status and does not require typing.

Many attorneys hire mature women who have raised their families. They find that these women are generally stable and reliable, and are more likely to remain in a job for a longer period of time than someone younger.

Also, by enrolling in a paralegal program, you will be gaining knowledge of the business world. Some women who graduate from paralegal programs choose a career such as personnel, but are still able to utilize some of their paralegal training.

I am retiring soon and am considering a second career as a paralegal. Has this been done before?

This is an excellent field to enter when you retire since you can become trained as a legal assistant in a short period of time. Many law firms who need a paralegal for informational interviewing seek someone who has had previous work experience and is able to relate well to their older clients.

When I graduate from a paralegal program, will I be a certified paralegal? Is there a state examination similar to a bar examination for attorneys which a paralegal must take?

Paralegal programs issue either college degrees, diplomas, or certificates to those who have successfully completed their studies in a paralegal curriculum. These programs will be accredited by state agencies who make sure that the educational standards are sufficiently high. However, there have been no standard paralegal education curricula set up by these agencies.

The only type of accreditation available at this point is the approval granted by the American Bar Association. This approval is not mandatory for a paralegal program to operate effectively. A program will make a request for approval and must follow the guidelines set forth by the ABA to receive the approval. State bar associations and paralegal associations may also set up their own guidelines for approving programs, and in the future this may become an alternate accreditation mechanism.

A certification examination is sponsored by the National

Association of Legal Assistants, Inc. (NALA). This is not a mandatory examination. Contact NALA directly for further information (see page 138 for address and phone number).

There is no state examination for paralegals such as the bar examination given to attorneys. Paralegal programs give their own examinations to their students based on their course content.

Should I take an internship as part of my paralegal training?

An internship experience can be an excellent supplement to your formal classroom training as a paralegal. Not all programs offer internships, instead requiring students to set up one for themselves.

In addition to being a clinical experience, it is something else to add to your résumé. You will also find that you may make contacts as an intern which can assist you in finding permanent employment.

However, an internship can take 10–15 hours a week—time away from your studying and class assignments.

It is best to weigh all the advantages and disadvantages before committing yourself. It is truly an individual choice to make.

What kind of financial aid is available for paralegal students?

This varies from state to state and from program to program. Some programs may offer scholarships and loans. You should contact the individual program for this information.

When choosing a program, how important is American Bar Association approval?

American Bar Association approval is a voluntary effort initiated by the paralegal program. When you are evaluating and comparing paralegal programs you should be considering both the type of program (baccalaureate degree, associate degree, certificate, or diploma), and the law library, faculty, and placement assistance.

Since the American Bar Association approval signifies certain high legal standards set by the ABA, attorneys will often rather employ graduates of ABA approved programs.

Do law schools accept paralegal courses for transfer credit?

No. Law school is a completely separate entity from paralegal schools. There is no transfer of credit.

I am a legal secretary who graduated from a paralegal program. Now that I have paralegal training I no longer want to type. What do I say at the job interview when I am asked if I will type on the job? Will I have to take a salary cut?

Many legal secretaries take paralegal programs to upgrade their positions. Since this is common, most employers of paralegals are aware that some of their applicants will have paralegal training as well as excellent secretarial skills.

First, it is important to realize that many legal secretaries in major law firms have higher salaries than those of paralegals. In fact, a legal secretary with excellent skills can command a salary in the mid-twenties in a large corporate law firm. The reason for this is that his/her skills are *measurable*, whereas paralegal skills are conceptual and procedural.

You can point out to a prospective employer that you have gone through a fairly rigorous program of study and paid tuition to become a paralegal, and that like most people who go through that type of training, you are anxious to use your new skills.

A large law practice cannot use a paralegal effectively if the paralegal types for the attorneys as well as performs paralegal work. Therefore, most of these offices have legal secretaries in addition to paralegals, and often have typing pools to handle the typing.

A smaller firm, sole practitioner, or a legal aid organization may not have the financial resources to employ both a paralegal and several secretaries. Someone with both paralegal training and good secretarial skills would be an asset to such a practice, and you might be hired over someone who did not have typing skills. I suggest that you inquire if the typing you would handle would be yours only or also include the lawyers' typing.

When there is a dearth of paralegal positions open in your

geographic area, you may have to settle for a job where your paralegal and typing skills are both utilized. Remember, though, you are not wedded to a job, and after gaining valuable experience, you can always move on.

Is there part-time work for paralegals?

There is some part-time employment available for paralegals; however, it is dependent on the size of the law firm as well as the type of law practiced. A smaller law firm or a sole practitioner may find that hiring a paralegal to work two or three times a week suits their needs. Usually this kind of practice will be in probate, estates and trusts, or matrimonial law.

For your first job as a paralegal, you are better off seeking a full-time position; there will be more positions open. After you have worked awhile and gained some experience, you will be able to seek part-time employment or negotiate for such a position with your employer.

The lawyers I work for want to train me in a different area of law from the one I studied. What should I do?

A paralegal training program is merely an introduction to law. Within a classroom setting there is only so much material which can be taught. When you graduate from a program, you will have attained skills which can be applied to other areas of law as well as in other careers. The more you know, the more marketable you will become.

If you have the opportunity to become trained in another area of law, by all means do so. You will find that all law is interrelated. Your formal classroom studies will always be of assistance to you while you are being "retrained" to work in another area of law.

What are some ethical considerations for paralegals?

The American Bar Association Code of Professional Responsibility and Canon of Judicial Ethics, Ethical Considerations 3-6

(1969) requires that a paralegal must be supervised by a lawyer. "A lawyer often delegates tasks to clerks, secretaries and other lay persons. Such delegation is proper if the lawyer maintains a direct relationship with his client, supervises the delegated work, and has complete professional responsibility for the work product. This delegation enables a lawyer to render legal services more economically and efficiently."

As a paralegal you will be performing work which requires legal judgment, but only an attorney admitted to the bar can give legal advice to a client, set the fee schedules, and appear in court.

The responsibilities that a lawyer will delegate to a paralegal will vary from law office to law office. Generally this is dependent on how experienced the paralegal is and how experienced the lawyer is in using a paralegal. For example, some lawyers will allow paralegals to do legal research, others will not. Some lawyers in states where paralegals are allowed to be advocates will allow the paralegals to represent their clients at administrative hearings, others will not.

Are there continuing education courses for paralegals working in the field?

Continuing education is a necessity for employed paralegals to ensure their competence and success in working in the legal community.

Continuing education courses are usually offered as one- to three-day seminars through legal assistant training programs, bar associations, and proprietary institutes whose function is to run continuing education courses for lawyers and paralegals.

Seminar topics may include: the paralegal's role in complex litigation, estate and gift tax laws, employee benefits laws, and Securities and Exchange Commission regulations. Other more specialized seminars may be developed for the preparation of federal fiduciary income taxes, postmortem estate planning, the management of computers and litigation support systems, and new developments in pension plan administration.

These seminars are also of interest to the novice paralegal who needs a "crash course" in learning a new area of law in addition to his/her paralegal education.

Can a paralegal have his/her own business card?

A paralegal may have business cards with the firm's name appearing on it. His/her status as a legal assistant must be clear.

How does a paralegal sign his/her correspondence?

A paralegal must never represent himself/herself as an attorney. He/she may sign his/her name on the letterhead stationery of the law firm when he/she identifies himself/herself as a paralegal or with any other title the firm has assigned to him/her.

2. Paralegal Training Programs

People who choose the paralegal profession usually have the following traits in common: They have good writing and verbal skills, they are intelligent, and they enjoy working with people. These characteristics are important because they are similar to what it takes to become a competent attorney.

A paralegal career is open to people with high school diplomas, legal secretarial experience, college degrees, or graduate degrees. It is important to choose the paralegal training program which is appropriate to your prior educational background and the employment opportunities available in your geographic area.

There are no prescribed high school courses or particular college majors required for entrance into paralegal programs. However, the ability to communicate well both orally and in writing is important in your success as a paralegal student and ultimately in your career. History, English, and foreign language courses are particularly useful in strengthening communication skills.

Paralegal training programs should view the paralegal's role as similar to that of the lawyer and in the delivery of legal services. In order for a paralegal to work effectively with an attorney, he/she must understand what an attorney does. Paralegal training programs should include in their curricula an overview of the activities in which a lawyer engages. Graduate paralegals will then have a basic understanding of the operation of a law office and have a better understanding of where and how they will fit into the legal community.

Prior to the inauguration of formal degree or certificate programs, paralegals were trained in-house. The in-house training programs for paralegals began on an ad hoc basis as the need for a paralegal developed. Usually it resulted from a small firm quickly expanding the scope of its practice, and wishing to train a competent legal secretary to perform paralegal duties. The legal secretary would then be able to incorporate his/her secretarial duties with the on-the-job paralegal training received from the lawyers.

The informal method of training a paralegal served the needs of a small law firm. But this kind of training is time-consuming for the attorney and can be haphazard. Paralegals may be trained

to perform certain tasks in the office, but they may not understand why. This can interfere with their ability to apply the
same principles in another case. The forms put together to serve
as a "training manual" for one type of case might not be
applicable to another case; one office's forms might be totally
inappropriate in another law office.

Nonetheless, legal secretaries were able to upgrade their
positions with in-house paralegal training programs, and until
formal programs developed, this was the only available education
for paralegals. However informal this training may have been,
it still offered a clinical education which provided the paralegal
with the opportunity to integrate his/her training with legal
experience.

Formal paralegal training began as the legal community recognized the need to provide a professional education to those people
interested in working as legal assistants. The strong need for
qualified paralegals developed in part from the need to provide
less expensive legal services to clients and also to assist attorneys
in an increasingly litigious society.

American Bar Association (ABA) Approval

At the present time there are over 300 paralegal training
institutions in the United States. As this book is being written,
68 of the programs are approved by the American Bar Association. In 1973 the American Bar Association issued certain
guidelines for approving paralegal training programs. Application may be made for either provisional or final approval.
Final approval becomes applicable when a program has been
operating for two years, and has graduated students.

The approval process involves the program preparing and
submitting a self-evaluation report, an on-site visitation by a
team of three members representing the ABA's Standing Committee on Legal Assistants, a review of the self-evaluation report
by the ABA staff and a consultant to the Standing Committee,
a review of the evaluation report made by the visitation team,
and a recommendation by the Committee to the ABA House of
Delegates for final approval.

Approval by the House of Delegates may be obtained at either
the ABA's annual (August) or midyear (February) meeting.

This approval is based on criteria set up by the ABA. Paralegal programs apply for the approval on a strictly voluntary basis. A program which does not have ABA approval because it could not financially afford to apply for the approval, or because it lacks certain facilities that the ABA requires in order to grant approval, may still follow the ABA's guidelines. An attorney interested in hiring a paralegal will be impressed if the applicant graduated from an American Bar Association approved program.

It is always a good idea for prospective paralegal students to personally evaluate programs on the basis of law library facilities, qualified instructors, curriculum internships available, and job placement assistance.

There are several different kinds of paralegal programs to choose from. Some require the applicants to have completed college, others only evaluate candidates on the basis of maturity and work experience. High school graduates will generally have to attain legal secretarial experience along with the paralegal certificate in order to gain employment as a legal assistant. Some combine training into an associate's or a bachelor's degree. Examples and descriptions of various types of programs and sample curricula will follow.

Attending a Paralegal Program

Most students feel a bit nervous before their first day of classes in a paralegal program. Many of the students may have been out of school for a number of years, others may have some anxiety about studying topics that are totally unfamiliar to them.

Remember that you are not alone with your feelings. The other students around you will probably have the same fears. But most importantly, remember that the instructors in the program will understand your feelings and not expect any of the students to have prior legal experience or knowledge, although some of the students may be legal secretaries or paralegals who have had on-the-job training. Of course these students will come into the classes with an understanding of some of the legal terminology.

Most programs will not guarantee their graduates a position upon their successful completion of the program, but a reputable program will offer some kind of job placement assistance to its students. When you evaluate programs, find out about their

Paralegal students sit through many hours of classroom instruction.

After class paralegal students spend time in the library completing assignments.

placement assistance and the kinds of contacts that the program has in the legal community.

The main feature to look for is an employment orientation that includes résumé writing for the legal community, job search techniques, and interviewing skills. Without these three basic components the graduate paralegal will find it difficult to look for his/her first legal assistant position.

Some programs, due to financial restrictions, may not have a thorough placement program, so this book includes some basic information about seeking a paralegal position.

Most paralegal programs supply their students with course materials consisting of outlines, forms, charts, and sample problems. Sometimes there is a charge for these materials. Students will usually purchase books that have been selected for use in the classes. Some of these books will be texts written especially for paralegal students, others will be law texts which are used in law school.

Paralegal programs will either have their own law libraries or have access to one. Students are expected to learn how to use the law library for the completion of their legal research assignments. Most law libraries have trained personnel available to assist students with these tasks. Students can expect both research and writing assignments while they are attending a paralegal program.

The faculty in a paralegal program will be attorneys and paralegals. These instructors may be employed full-time, part-time, or on an adjunct basis. A student should be able to make an appointment to meet with a professor after class if he/she is having difficulty with a particular legal concept or an assigned reading.

Generally assignments will be given out on a daily or weekly basis with some special projects due at the end of the semester. Often there are midterm and final examinations given in each course.

Upon successful completion of a program, a paralegal graduate will either receive a diploma or a degree and a transcript of his/her grades. The transcript may be taken along to job interviews, if necessary.

Plan for an hour's worth of studying for each hour you spend in the classroom. If you budget your time for studying and complete your assignments on time, you should have no problem graduating from a paralegal program.

Certificate Programs in Paralegal Studies for Students with a College Degree

Certificate programs in paralegal studies are noncredit and nondegree courses offered through colleges, universities, and proprietary schools. Some certificate programs require that the applicant possess a two-year or a four-year college degree before applying to the program. Many certificate programs require that the applicant have completed 45 college credits before applying to the program to ensure a general education. Others require only that the applicant be a mature individual sincerely interested in pursuing a career as a legal assistant.

Many of the programs which require a baccalaureate degree as one of the entrance requirements also require a personal interview, references, an essay, and high academic achievement in college work.

Certificate programs range in duration from three months to two years. Most college graduates prefer to take the three-month or six-month programs in order to prepare themselves in a short period of time to enter the paralegal profession.

The three- and six-month programs have very intensive curricula. They are offered as either a full-time day program or as a part-time evening program. Some programs offer specialized areas of law and others offer a general practice curriculum.

Daytime certificate programs generally appeal to people who are not working. Evening programs attract both employed and unemployed people.

Mercy College's American Bar Association approved certificate paralegal program, located in White Plains, New York, offers both a specialist and a generalist program for college graduates. Both curricula are over 200 hours in duration. The full-time, three-month day program's curriculum allows the students to choose one area of law to major in. The areas of specialization to choose from are: litigation and trial preparation, corporations and securities, real estate, probate, estates and trusts, and employee benefits. In addition, the students attend a legal research class once a week. This full-time program prepares its graduates to become specialists in one area of law. This is especially useful to the larger law firms or corporate legal departments in major metropolitan areas.

The evening program's curriculum is a general practice one where the student studies six areas of law. They are: matrimonial law, criminal law, business organization, litigation and trial preparation, real estate, and probate, estates and trusts. The student must also take legal research classes which meet every other Saturday. This part-time program takes six months to complete and prepares its graduates to become generalists. This preparation is particularly useful when working in smaller law firms and in less densely populated areas of the country.

Curriculum

Day Program

Core Curriculum (Part of both day and evening curriculum). Introduction to the paralegal profession; and law office management—an overview.

Employment Orientation (Part of both day and evening curriculum). Résumé preparation; counseling on interviewing strategy; and assistance in conducting the overall job search.

Legal Research (Part of both day and evening curriculum). Includes writing workshop and drafting of legal instruments.
   Functional skills acquired include a working knowledge of federal and state legislative documents including statute books and related legislative historical documents; federal and state case reporter systems; the hierarchy of the federal and state court systems; law digests; legal form books; looseleaf services; legal encyclopedia; case and state citators; legal treatises; legal periodicals; and both national and local standards of citation used in legal writing. Under supervision, the graduate will also be able to prepare a law office or trial memorandum, a trial court brief, and an appellate court brief.

Specialist Electives. The student selects one of the following areas as his/her Specialist Elective.

Litigation and Trial Preparation. Functional skills acquired include preparing and maintaining the file; gathering information through client interviews; drafting pleadings; organizing and indexing documents; tracing evidence; examining public records; and preparing briefs and memoranda. Client intake procedure; Preparing the file; Concepts of jurisdiction and venue; Parties to an action; Pleadings; Motion practice; Accelerated judgment; Pretrial discovery and disclosure; Trials; Judgments and their enforcement; Appeals; Special proceedings; and Provisional remedies.

Real Estate. Functional skills acquired include conducting title searches; assisting in preparation and drafting of deeds, contracts of sale, leases, and abstracts of title; gathering and reviewing documentation necessary in mortgage transactions; recording deeds and mortgages; organizing and notarizing documents at the closing. Introduction; Estates and real property; Liens and encumbrances; Transfer of title; Deeds, leases, and mortgages; Zoning; Real estate brokers; Contracts of sale; Closings; Surveys, title searches, and abstracts; Records and recording; Title reports; Foreclosure; and Condemnation.

Probate, Estates and Trusts. Functional skills acquired include assisting in preparation of legal documents associated with estate planning; collecting assets; notifying beneficiaries; preparing federal and state estate tax returns; submitting documentation to the Surrogate's Court for probate; transferring securities; drawing checks for the executor's signature; and maintaining account records.

Substantive. Overview; The will; Intestate succession; Probate proceedings; Administration proceedings; Ancillary administration; Temporary administration and preliminary; Letters testamentary; Estate administration; Powers of fiduciary; Accounting; and Trusts.

Taxation. Estate, income, gift taxation: Overview; Federal estate tax; New York estate tax; The gift tax; Fiduciary tax return: Form 1041; and Decedent's final income tax return: Form 1040.

Corporations and Securities. Functional skills acquired include preparing articles of incorporation; satisfying state filing requirements; taking minutes at board of director's meetings; preparing necessary documentation for mergers and new acquisitions; and preparation of registration materials for regulatory agencies. Introduction: Types of business organizations; Reasons for using the corporate form of organization; Organizing the corporation; Capital structure; Operating the corporation; Directors and officers; Distributions to stockholders; Stockholder derivative lawsuits; Antitrust laws; Mergers or consolidations of corporations; Operating in other states; Going public; Operating a publicly owned corporation; Understanding financial statements; and Liquidation and dissolution.

Employee Benefits. Functional skills acquired include preparing all filing requirements established by ERISA for installation and amendment of deferred compensation plans; preparing summary plan descriptions; interfacing with sponsors, administrators, trustees, employers, and other parties; and assisting with the drafting of documentation necessary for plan formation. Overview of ERISA and other employee benefits; Concepts of deferred compensation plans; certain fundamental requisites of qualified plans and trusts; Coverage and discrimination; Contributions and benefits; Defined contribution plans; Participation; funding, and vesting; Administration; Integration of plans with Social Security; Discontinuance, partial termination of plans; Individual retirement accounts and Keogh Plans; and Taxability of distribution from qualified plans.

Evening Program

Students in the evening program must complete the general practice curriculum which includes study of all the following legal areas.

Business Organizations (30 hours). Common characteristics and distinctions among proprietorships, partnerships, and corporations; Emphasis will be on corporations, with discussion of formation and financial structure; Rights of stockholders; Officers and directors; Mergers and consolidations; Foreign corporations; Publicly owned corporations; Accounting concepts and financial statements; and Liquidation and dissolution.

Probates, Estates and Trusts (36 hours). Introduction to estate administration probate proceedings; Collection of assets; Appraisals; Liquidity; and Disposition of real property; Federal and state taxation; Testamentary trusts; Accountings and final distribution; and Planning and drafting of wills.

Litigation and Trial Preparation (36 hours). Initial client interview and case preparation; Jurisdiction; Parties to an action; Summons and pleadings; Pretrial obtaining of evidence; Motion practice; Provisional remedies; Preparation for trial; Judgments and their enforcement; Appeals; and Closing the file.

Real Estate (30 hours). Transfer of title to real property; Mortgages and foreclosures; Leases; Deeds; Zoning; Recording; Title searches; Surveys; Closings; Contracts of sale; Liens and their enforcement; Condemnation; and Real estate brokers.

Matrimonial Law (12 hours). The marriage contract; Spouse's rights and obligations; Void and voidable marriages; Annulment; Separation; Divorce; Support and alimony; and Custody of children.

Criminal Law (12 hours). The initial interview; Bail; Arraignment; Preliminary hearing; The grand jury; Motions; Discovery; Jury selection; Case for the prosecution and presentation of the defense; Summation; and Post trial procedure.

Note: The course descriptions have been obtained from Mercy College's Paralegal Program's brochure.

Diploma and Certificate Programs for Students without a College Degree

For those with no college degree or with 45 hours or more of general education credits from college, there are other types of certificate and diploma programs available for paralegal training. These nondegree programs are offered through colleges, universities, and proprietary schools.

Requirements for admission vary from program to program, but a minimum of a high school diploma, or equivalency, with ability to handle college level work is mandatory. Most attorneys do prefer to hire paralegals with some college background. Persons without at least forty-five college credits (the equivalent of one-and-a-half years of college) should consider supplementing their paralegal training with other undergraduate courses.

The type of training received in a diploma or certificate program will prepare students to work in large metropolitan areas in law firms, corporations, courts, and the government. The Division of Continuing Education of Oakland University in Rochester, Michigan, offers a legal assistant program for both credit and noncredit. This American Bar Association approved program offers courses in the evening on a noncredit basis and for credit to the University's undergraduates through the political science department.

Applicants must also pass a Personal Assessment Inventory for basic necessary skills. This consists of a series of three tests indicating language skills and levels of abstract reasoning, and submission of a one-page, typed autobiography.

If a student has also completed 45 hours or more of undergraduate academic credit at an accredited institution or the equivalent, he/she is awarded a diploma. Only the diploma program is approved by the ABA.

Objectives, course content, and instruction are identical in each legal assistant class for all enrollees.

Curriculum[1]

Foundation Courses

The Diploma Certificate Program for Legal Assistants begins with the following five required foundation courses which should be completed before enrollment in concentration courses.

---

[1] *Courtesy of Oakland University. From their legal assistant's program brochure.*

Introduction to the Law. An introductory course to facilitate a better understanding of the law, the legal process, and the operation of the judicial system.

Roles of a Legal Assistant. An orientation course to widen understanding of the variety of roles, opportunities, professional responsibilities, problems, and physical settings encountered by legal assistants to enable students to acquire knowledge about the legal profession and to wisely select a concentration. Includes a presentation by practicing legal assistants.

Substantive Law. Overview of the elements of tort, contract, and property law and the development of fundamental skills in recognizing substantive issues in practical law office situations.

Legal Research and Writing. Acquiring essential skills in legal research and legal writing by means of a variety of exercises culminating in a legal memorandum, students will develop their ability to analyze, interpret, and communicate facts and ideas. This course introduces students to the law library and state law. Introduction to the Law is a prerequisite. Four sessions of this course meet at the Oakland County Law Library.

Principles of Accounting. An introduction to accounting theory with emphasis on the accounting principles used to prepare books of original entry and their relationship to the preparation of financial statements. Through lectures, class discussion, and problem solving, students are exposed to the complete accounting cycle from recognition and recording of business transactions to preparation of financial statements and the relationship of the accounting and legal professions.

Concentration Courses

Following completion of the foundation courses, enrollees elect one of three concentrations, each of which require from five to six additional, specialized courses, general practice concentration, litigation concentration, and probate administration and estate planning concentration. Legal Research and Writing II is offered every term. Other concentration courses are offered every other term.

Legal Research and Writing II. Required for the general practice and litigation concentrations. A continuation of the beginning course dealing with various kinds of specialized legal research and including legal writing relating to federal law.

General Practice Concentration

Real Property Transactions. Overview of all phases of real property transactions; preparing and recording documents for transfer of title, making title searches and reports, preparing deeds and mortgages, lease drafting, settlements, and closings.

Estates and Trusts. Overview of various methods of transferring assets, including gifts, wills, and trusts, and the review of typical documents. Study of administration of decedents' estates including probate procedures, federal and state death taxes, income taxes, and fiduciary accounting and responsibilities.

Corporations. A comparison of the sole proprietorship, partnership, and corporate forms of business organization with stress upon the corporate form; substantive examination of corporate structure and organization; drafting articles and by-laws; conducting the corporate business; and issuing equity and debt securities.

Litigation. An overview of case preparation before trial including an examination of the various procedures to be completed and the documents to be filed; working up trial documents for counsel's assistance.

Paralegal Programs Associated with Law Schools

A paralegal program associated with a law school offers its students the opportunity to be exposed to a law school setting while they are studying to become paralegals. This is particularly advantageous for a person considering law school as the next step after completing his/her paralegal degree. There is no guarantee, however, that a paralegal will be accepted into that law school.

These programs are open to high school graduates with acceptable college board scores as well as those with bachelor's degrees. An accelerated paralegal program may be offered to college graduates enabling them to complete the same program in one year rather than the two years that it would take high school graduates. High school graduates would be required to take four semesters of general education and legal courses for a total of sixty credits leading to an associate degree in paralegal studies. College graduates would be required to take only legal courses which could be completed in two semesters. Some paralegal programs offered through law schools may be certificate programs, not offering associate degrees for those with no college education.

In addition to being in a law school environment, other unique advantages in attending a paralegal program associated with a law school are the excellent law library facilities, the opportunity to attend all the law school's seminars and outside lectures offered through Continuing Legal Education, and some additional placement assistance through the law school.

The Legal Assistant Program at the University of Bridgeport is associated with the University of Bridgeport School of Law. Their curriculum follows.

Course Descriptions[1]

(Number in parentheses indicates credits given for courses. Asterisks identify courses which would be waived for a college graduate)

First-Year Program: First Semester Curriculum

*Composition and Rhetoric** (3). An introduction to the elements of effective writing, concentration on structure, logic, specificity,

---

[1] *Courtesy of the University of Bridgeport. From their legal assistant program brochure.*

focus, grammar, sentence structure, and mechanics. Frequent writing in and out of class. By the end of the semester, students should be able to compose an organized, grammatically correct, and adequately developed expository essay.

Criminal Law and Torts (3). A survey of general principles of criminal law, defenses, court procedures, and jurisdiction. A general overview of torts, the nature of a tort, who may be liable, and the extent of liability and defenses. Emphasis is placed upon the practical application of this knowledge for the paralegal. This course must be taken in conjunction with Legal Research 1.

Legal Research 1 (3). An introduction to the study of law which acquaints the student with analysis and synthesis of cases and other legal materials. The student is taught to use various methods of legal research, which includes indexes, digests, Shepard's Citations, encyclopedias, and the West Key number system. Each student is required to submit a written abstract and legal memoranda on problems involving questions of substantive law procedure and legal ethics. This course must be taken in conjunction with Criminal Law and Torts.

Fundamentals of Management (3). Fundamentals of production/ operations management, planning, organizing, and controlling the process of producing goods and services. Major topics include facility location and layout, work simplification and work measurement, productions and inventory planning and control systems, quality control systems and project management. Quantitative decision-making models are stressed.

*Liberal Arts Elective (3)

Semester Total: 15

Second Semester Curriculum

*Composition and Rhetoric (3). Emphasis on the writing of the formal analytical essay and the essential methods of research common to various academic disciplines. Close readings of a broad range of fiction and essays. By the end of the semester, students should demonstrate a mastery of the formal essay and the research paper.

Contracts and Uniform Commercial Code (3). A general survey of contract law, definitions and classifications of contracts; capacity of parties; legal effect of offer, acceptance, and consideration. Uniform Commercial Code—definition; consideration of problems affecting Article 2 of the Code—sales; definitions, consideration of the problems affecting Article 3—commercial paper; definitions and consideration of problems affecting Article 4—bank deposits and collections (negotiable instruments); definitions and consideration affecting Article 9—secured transactions. This course must be taken in conjunction with Legal Writing. Prerequisites: Criminal Law and Torts, Legal Research 1.

Legal Writing (3). To give the paralegal a working knowledge of the Connecticut Rules of Practice and Procedure. Heavy emphasis is placed on learning to draft pleadings, motions, memoranda of law, and appellate briefs. In addition, the Code of Professional Responsibility is examined through class discussion and hypothetical examples. This course must be taken in conjunction with Contracts and U.C.C. Prerequisites: Criminal Law, Torts, and Legal Research 1.

*Introduction to Psychology (3). The scientific study of human behavior through consideration of basic methods, findings, and theories in such areas as learning, motivation, emotion, personality, and social behavior. Applications made to personal adjustment.

*Liberal Arts Elective (3)

Semester Total: 15

Third Semester Curriculum

Business Organizations and Domestic Relation (3). A general overview of the law of business organizations; formation operation, and dissolution of partnerships, corporations, and limited partnerships are studied with emphasis on the practical application of this body of knowledge in the law office. A survey of domestic relations, marriage, dissolution of marriage, separation agreements, custody, alimony, and child support are studied. Prerequisites: Contracts, U.C.C., and Legal Writing.

Property and Conveyancing (3). An introduction to the law of real and personal property; nature of property, possession, and its consequences; acquisition of property and transfer. A study of practical problems involving conveyances from the drafting of purchase and sale agreements to the passing of papers; mechanics of the title examination; mortgages and foreclosure. Prerequisites: Contracts, U.C.C., and Legal Writing.

*General Accounting (3). Development of principles and procedures underlying financial statements. The elements of an accounting system, deemphasizing specialized record-keeping techniques and procedures. Stress in all discussions on the development and use of data for managerial control.

*Communication (3). Public communication. The process and variables of everyday public address are examined through situations, content, presentation strategies and effects, and by classroom practice in the basic principles of oral communication (two periods and laboratory).

*Liberal Arts Elective (3)

Semester Total: 15

Fourth Semester Curriculum

*Legal Office Procedures, Insurance, and Related Forms (3). A study of the work flow in a law office. Responsibilities in handling written communications and maintaining files; preparation of court documents; law office accounting, billing, and forms. Understanding the basic concepts of insurance law. An internship may be taken as an alternative with special permission of the director. (Life–Work Experience credits are available to legal secretaries.) Prerequisites: Contracts, U.C.C., and Legal Writing.

Estate, Probate, and Taxation (3). Students will be introduced to the basic concepts of estate and trust law, emphasis upon creation and administration of same. Definitions, consideration of problems, relative to the disposition of property; impact of federal income, inheritance, and estate and gift tax will be discussed. Prerequisites: Contracts, U.C.C., and Legal Writing.

General Accounting II (3). Managerial uses of cost data derived from job order, process, and standard cost accounting systems. Prerequisite: Accounting I.

* **Liberal Arts Electives (6)**

Semester Total: 15

Associate in Science Degree in Paralegal Studies (60 Credits)

Associate degree programs in paralegal studies generally offer a curriculum which will prepare graduates to work in general practice law firms.

This type of paralegal degree is offered through four-year undergraduate institutions granting bachelor's degrees, as well as two-year community colleges offering associate degrees. Entrance into many of the associate degree programs in paralegal studies is highly selective. Admissions committees seek students who have attained above average grades in high school, or students with bachelors' degrees who have demonstrated high academic achievement in their college courses.

Some programs require that applicants pass special aptitude tests given by the college's admissions department and paralegal program. Most programs request personal interviews, an essay, and written references. The reason for these prerequisites is to ensure that the paralegal student will be able to successfully complete the program which will consist of general education courses, electives, and legal specialty courses.

Many of these programs may be incorporated into bachelor degree programs.

Sacred Heart University in Bridgeport, Connecticut offers an American Bar Association approved two-year program leading to an associate in science degree in paralegal studies. Its legal assistant program is under the jurisdiction of the Department of Business Administration and is an example of a four-semester sequence which will train a student to become a legal assistant.

Course Descriptions[1]

First-Year Program

(Number in parentheses indicates credits given for course)

Freshman Rhetoric: Shorter Forms (3). A systematic and practical introduction to the techniques of effective writing. The course stresses the rudiments of the traditional rhetoric, and provides supervised practice in the writing of essays.

Criminal Law and Torts (3). A survey of general principles of criminal law defenses, court procedures, and jurisdiction; torts, the nature of a tort, who may be liable, the extent of liability and defenses. Emphasis is placed upon the practical application of this knowledge for the paralegal.

Legal Research I (3). An introduction to the study of law which acquaints the student with analysis and synthesis of cases and other legal materials. The student is taught to use various

[1] *Courtesy of Sacred Heart University. From their legal assistant program brochure.*

methods of legal research, which include indexes, digests, Shepard's Citations, encyclopedias, and the West Key number system. Each student is required to submit a written abstract and legal memoranda on problems involving questions of substantive law procedure and legal ethics.

Business: Its Nature and Environment (3). This basic introductory course is required of all business majors. It is concerned with the traditional facets of business as well as the social and physical climate in which business operates. The management point of view is emphasized, but the rights of the individual as employee, citizen, and consumer are also discussed. The purpose of the course is to provide a clear overview of the area of activity known as business. (Organization Management may be substituted if student has appropriate background.)

Liberal Arts Elective (3)

Semester Total: 15

Freshman Rhetoric: Longer Forms (3). A continuation of English 111. This course deals with the writing of argumentative-expository essays and the application of advanced rhetorical principles. Training in basic research methods is stressed.

Contracts and Uniform Commercial Code (3). A general survey of contract law, definitions and classifications of contracts; capacity of parties; legal effect of offer, acceptance and consideration, Uniform Commercial Code—definition; consideration of problems affecting Article 2 of the Code—sales; definitions, consideration of the problems affecting Article 3—commercial paper; definitions and consideration of problems affecting Article 4—bank deposits and collections (negotiable instruments); definitions and consideration affecting Article 9—secured transactions.

Legal Research II (3). A working knowledge of the Connecticut Rules of Practice and Procedure. Heavy emphasis is placed on learning to draft pleadings, motions, memoranda of law, and appellate briefs. In addition the Code of Professional Responsibility is examined through class discussion and hypothetical examples.

Applied Psychology (3). A survey of the professional activities of psychologists as applied to the fields of business, advertising, mental health, education, and law.

Liberal Arts Elective (3)

Semester Total: 15

Second-Year Program: First Semester

Business Organizations and Domestic Relations (3). A general overview of the law of business organizations; formation, operation, and dissolution of partnerships, corporations, and limited partnerships are studied with emphasis on the practical application of this body of knowledge in the law office. The principles of agency law are also covered.

To give the student a broad background in the field of domestic relations; marriage, dissolution of marriage, separation agreements, custody, alimony, and child support are studied.

Property and Conveyancing (3). An introduction to the law of real and personal property; nature of property, possession and its consequences; acquisition of property and transfer. A study of practical problems involving conveyances from the drafting of purchase and sale agreements to the passing of papers; mechanics of the title examination; mortgages and foreclosure.

Accounting for Managers I (3). Presentation and explanation of the functions of financial accounting. Emphasizing the practical uses of accounting data, it is designed to enable the nonaccountant to read financial statements intelligently and to make use of the information contained therein.

Effective Communication (3). Introductory instruction and practice in effective oral self-expressions; working with ideas and emotions as found in selected projects in speaking and oral reading.

Liberal Arts Elective (3)

Semester Total: 15

Second-Year Program: Second Semester

Legal Office Procedures, Insurance, and Related Forms (3). A study of the work flow in a law office. Responsibilities in handling written communications and maintaining files; preparation of court documents; law office accounting, billing, and forms. Understanding the basic concepts of insurance law. An internship may be taken as an alternative with special permission of the director. (Life–Work Experience credits are available to legal secretaries.)

Estates, Probate, and Taxation (3). Students will be introduced to the basic concepts of estate and trust law, emphasis upon creation and administration of same. Definitions, consideration of problems relative to the disposition of property; impact of federal income, inheritance, and estate and gift tax will be discussed.

Accounting for Managers II (3). Continuation of Accounting for Managers I. Emphasis on managerial accounting.

Liberal Arts Electives (6)

Semester Total: 15

Program Total: 60

Baccalaureate Degree in Paralegal Studies (120 Credits)

Some colleges and universities offer majors or minors in paralegal studies, depending upon the school. A student would graduate with a B.A. or a B.S. in paralegal studies or legal studies.

A baccalaureate degree program prepares the student for work in a law-related environment as well as furnishing a liberal arts education. These degree programs are not designed to be prelaw programs nor do they make any attempt to guarantee placement into law school. They do offer liberal arts courses, business courses, and a paralegal specialty curriculum. These four-year programs may combine both a generalist and a specialist legal studies program. Many of these programs also offer law office administration courses.

Admittance into baccalaureate degree paralegal programs is usually based on the college's general entrance criteria. In addition, the legal studies department may have special requirements, such as an interview with the chairman of the department. Career opportunities for graduates of four-year paralegal programs are in law firms, corporations, and government.

The Legal Studies Department at Quinnipiac College in Hamden, Connecticut, is a bachelor of arts program with a major in legal studies. In this American Bar Association approved 120-semester–hour curriculum, the legal studies major is required to enroll in a variety of liberal arts and business courses and encouraged to minor or concentrate in related areas of study, for example, accounting, political science, and history.

All majors are required to complete a two-semester internship in their senior year. Supervised placements, which are arranged according to the individual interests of the students, are available in law firms, government agencies, and corporate legal departments.

To complete the bachelor's degree in legal studies, students must take accounting, English, history, and sociology courses. Within the major area, students must complete a proseminar in legal studies, introduction to the American legal system, library methods in the law, civil procedure I and II, legal writing, law office management, and the legal internship. In addition, the legal studies major must take at least four electives from selected offerings in legal studies and partnerships and corporations, three of which must be at the 300 level or higher. With agreement of their advisors, students must also complete a minor or concentration which is related to their professional goals.

The following are descriptions of the courses in the Legal Studies and Law Departments at Quinnipiac College.

Course Descriptions[1]

Legal Studies (Numbers in parentheses indicate credit given for course.)

Proseminar in Legal Studies (1). An introduction to the Legal Studies Program and to important issues facing legal assistants. Issues to be covered include legal ethics and authorized practice, law office management and the legal assistant functions of the legal assistant, and the court system.

Introduction to the American Legal System (3). Introduction to basic legal concepts and the structure of the American court system as well as legal theory and procedure, and an overview of law.

Library Methods in the Law (3). Introduction to the use of the law library. How to move from a fact situation, through the sources of legal authority, to the application of the law to the specific facts. Course will include a discussion of the bases of legal authority as well as practical library skills. Sources: codes and administrative regulations, reporters and digests, encyclopedias, citators, law reviews, and treatises. Given at the Yale Law School Library.

Criminal Justice I (3). Overview of the American system of criminal justice, including study of its various institutions, such as the criminal courts, police, prosecutors and defense attorneys, and jails and prisons. Study of the Fourth Amendment (search and seizure) and the Fifth Amendment (privilege against self-incrimination). Also explored are schools of thought underlying criminal prosecution and correctional philosophy.

Civil Procedures I, II (6). Comprehensive study of pleadings and procedures in civil proceedings with special emphasis on drafting

[1] *Courtesy of Quinnipiac College. From their legal studies program brochure and general college catalogue.*

of complaints, responsive pleadings, discovery motions, and responses.

Legal Writing (3). Development of legal writing skills. Emphasis on precision and clarity in writing; legal citation and format. Drafting of letters and memoranda of law.

Law Office Management. Introduction to the intricacies of running a law office. Areas covered include law office systems and controls (information retrieval systems, docket control, substantive law systems); office personnel; client relations; law office equipment (word processing, communications systems).

Administrative Agencies (3). Introduction to the workings of, and procedures involved in dealing with government agencies. Skills involved in being an advocate are covered.

Topics in the Law (3). Designed to introduce students to a specific area of the law; to perfect legal research, writing, and communication skills, and to involve students in serving the local community. Students will research an area of the law, prepare legal memoranda, and make presentations to local high school classes. Specific topics will be announced each semester; for example, family law, law affecting the elderly, rights of the handicapped.

Probate and Estate Administration (3). Review of probate law. Students will generate forms and other instruments related to modern probate practice.

Land Transfer and Closing Procedures (3). Background for the sources of real estate law, land and its elements, and land titles and interest in land; procedures for conveying interests in land, recording statutes, and searching titles. Emphasis given to the preparation, coordination, and completion of real estate closings.

Legal Internship I, II (8). Supervised placement in a law firm, agency, or corporate legal department as a legal worker, for

10 hours a week along with a weekly seminar where students meet to talk about their work, their roles, their challenges, the problems of being a nonlawyer in the legal profession, and to work on various skills necessary for an advocate. Prerequisite: Senior standing.

Partnerships and Corporations (3). Nature and kinds of partnerships. Relationships between partners, and between partners and third persons. Causes and effects of partnership dissolutions. Promotion and organization of corporations. Corporate powers. Relationship of stockholders and creditors to the corporation and of the corporation to the state.

Master's Degree in Legal Studies

For persons wishing to supplement their paralegal training program with a master's degree, there are Master of Arts programs in legal studies available. Persons who take these programs may or may not have prior paralegal education or experience, although a college degree or senior year status is usually required.

People wishing to take a master's degree in legal studies are seeking legal skills to assist them in management and executive positions. Some students also consider applying to law school after completion of this degree.

An example of such a program is that available at the Antioch School of Law, Center for Legal Studies, in Washington, D.C. Their program takes from one year to fifteen months to complete. It is a two-stage program: Stage One consists of the Winter Intensive Legal Skills Program and includes courses in legal analysis, writing, and research, civil procedure, and evidence. Stage Two consists of an independent study/internship with options in employment discrimination law, insurance law, and public sector law.

The Law School Admission Test and the Graduate Record Examination Aptitude test are not required.

Canadian Law Clerks

Canada has its own version of the paralegal. A law clerk is a trained legal specialist who works under the general supervision of a barrister and/or solicitor. The law clerk who works in a small law office would be required to work as a generalist. The larger law offices would have the law clerk specialize in one area of the law. Like the American paralegal, the law clerk is able to handle routine legal and administrative matters in a law office. The Law Society in Canada and that country's legal community recognize the law clerk as being a valuable member of the legal profession.

Law clerks work in local, provisional, and federal governments. They also are employed in the legal departments of trust companies.

Seneca College of Applied Arts and Technology in Willowdale, Ontario, offers a law clerks program through its Continuing Education Division. This program is open to those who have completed grade 12 and have legal experience.

Four courses are offered in this program: real estate, probate and estate, corporate law, and litigation. A summary of the type of work entailed is as follows:

Real Estate

This concerns the purchase, sale, leasing, and mortgaging of land and buildings, and a law clerk would be concerned with the preparation and approval of the contract between the vendor and purchaser, the investigation of title, the preparation and completion of the necessary deeds and documents, details of the financing, closing of the transaction, and accounting to the client. It would require knowledge of all aspects of the law relating to real estate including familiarization with the applicable statutes and regulations.

Probate and Estates

This deals with the preparation of wills, estate planning, and the processing of the estate upon the death of a client. The work

would include ascertaining details of the assets and liabilities of the deceased, preparation of the various forms for the Surrogate Court and the provincial and federal authorities to obtain probate or letters of administration, attending to the administration and distribution of the estate, the preparation of accounts, etc. In this field, it would be necessary to be conversant with the laws relating to wills, trusts, taxation estates, and the procedures of the appropriate courts and revenue authorities.

Corporate Law

This involves the preparation and filing of applications for incorporation of companies and completion of their organization, the preparation and filing of documents in connection with variations in the constitution of companies, wind-up, registration in other jurisdictions, convening of meetings, attendance thereat, preparation of agenda and minutes, preparation and filing of returns, prospectuses and statements under the Securities Act and the various Stock Exchange forms, statements, returns, etc. Here it is necessary to be familiar with the provisions of the many statutes and regulations governing the formation and operation of corporations.

Litigation

Before any criminal, tortious, or contractual matter reaches trial in court the law clerk may be faced with a wide variety of duties including interviewing the client and witness, investigations, preparation of pleadings and briefs, in addition to preparation for and assisting at the trial itself.

The law clerk must have a thorough knowledge of the judicial system and its procedural requirements together with an understanding of the law pertaining to his/her particular field.

For further information regarding this program, write to:

Program Coordinator
Continuing Education Division
Markham Information Centre

Seneca College of Applied Arts and Technology
3 Centre Street
Markham, Ontario L3P 3P
Canada

For further information regarding law clerks, write to:

The Secretary
The Institute of Law Clerks of Ontario
Suite 12
347 Bay Street
Toronto, Ontario
Canada

3. The Work—Responsibilities, Growth Opportunities, and Environment

As mentioned in Chapter 1, the kinds of jobs and types of work settings for paralegals are as varied as those for attorneys. As we have mentioned already, law firms, corporations, insurance companies, pension consulting firms, banks, consulting firms, government, courthouses, legal aid societies, and legal corporations are some of the places that an entry-level paralegal might seek employment after his/her formal training. There are also other kinds of employment opportunities for paralegals which will be discussed in Chapter 7. Paralegals are working in large urban areas, small towns, suburban communities, and even from their own homes. When choosing a paralegal training program it is important to consider the type of law practice that you would prefer and to find a program which will prepare you for such work.

There are many points you must consider when looking for a job. You will have to decide on the size of the firm you prefer, the kind of law you are interested in, and what you are qualified to do.

Before applying for a paralegal position, it is best to do some research on the law firm or company in question to familiarize yourself with its background. Then you will have an idea of the kind of law being practiced which will help you be effective during the job interview. It is also a courtesy to the interviewer.

Private and Public Sectors

The private sector includes law firms, banks, corporations, and insurance companies. (The fees paid by clients generate the income of the legal office.) The kinds of law generally practiced in the private sector include corporate; antitrust; civil and criminal litigation; real estate; tax; probate, estates, and trusts; and matrimonial law.

The public sector includes agencies funded by federal, state, and local governments. The public sector agencies work on domestic, environmental, criminal, landlord–tenant, and consumer cases. There are also nonprofit organizations such as the ACLU which are privately funded. And the Legal Services Corporation which provides federal funds for legal aid programs for the poor nationwide.

Some of the major kinds of employers of paralegals, with their work settings, paralegal responsibilities, and job profiles from practicing paralegals will follow.

Law Firms

Law firms are the major employers of paralegals. A 1978 *National Law Journal* survey of the country's 100 largest law firms showed that 94 percent of the firms employed from 4 to 136 paralegals.

Some law firms may still have their own paralegal training programs with their own training manuals. This type of training is being phased out since it has proven to be too costly for such firms to hire paralegals without a formal paralegal education. In most cases, a graduate paralegal will still be trained in some specialized legal procedures that his/her employer requires but are not taught in a paralegal program.

Large law firms are those with over sixty attorneys, medium-sized firms have from twenty to fifty-nine attorneys, and small firms have fewer than twenty attorneys. The size of the law firm and type of practice is determined by the number of attorneys they employ. There are small, medium, and large firms in most major cities throughout the United States. In less densely populated areas of the country there may be only small law firms and sole practitioners.

Large Law Firms

The large firms, located in large cities, are departmentalized with a partner in charge of each specialty. In firms over sixty attorneys, there are usually departments for litigation, labor law, real estate, corporate, tax, and trusts and estates, etc. Sometimes a matter received in one department will need the assistance of another department. An example of this might be a labor law matter which requires litigation. Both the labor and litigation departments would work jointly on the case. A litigation paralegal would have to be trained in-house in labor law in order to work effectively on the matter.

The clients of large law firms are generally corporations, banks, insurance companies, and brokerage houses. The firm can also serve the needs of individuals seeking legal assistance in real estate, tax, and estate matters. Three or four paralegals will usually share an office and the services of a typist.

The tasks performed by a paralegal in a large firm can be routine and very systemized. Many law cases involve a voluminous number of documents, and it is a paralegal who will catalog, index, and summarize them. In nearly all of the large firms, paralegals will be supervised by the more experienced attorneys and paralegals, since the inexperienced associate will not know the kinds of tasks that can be routinely assigned to the paralegal.

Paralegals in these corporate firms will generally not perform legal research in the law library. Many of these firms, however, have computerized legal research equipment. A paralegal may be trained to operate it and in this instance a paralegal will assist in legal research.

The large law firms will usually treat their paralegals as professionals, including them in the firm's social functions. The paralegals are expected to attend department meetings and accompany attorneys to depositions and court. They are also expected to work overtime and travel as a case may demand.

There are distinct advantages in working as a paralegal in a large law firm. You will receive excellent benefits, including insurance, health, and three to four weeks paid vacation a year. You will become exposed to a wide variety of corporate clients and their businesses. Not only will you become familiar with the kinds of law the firm practices, but you will be making contacts that might be useful if you should wish to leave the firm after a few years.

Profile—Working in a Large Law Firm

In 1979 Mitchell B. graduated from college with a Bachelor of Science degree in management science. In his senior year of college he took both the business and law boards, did well in both of them and remained undecided on whether to attend law school or graduate business school. Since he had previously worked one summer in a business setting, he decided to look for a job as a paralegal to help him decide which kind of graduate training he would prefer.

Without a certificate from a paralegal training program he found it very difficult to even get an interview for a legal position. He hand delivered over 100 résumés to law firms before he was asked in for one interview.

He realized that it was going to take a lot of perseverance and time to eventually land a paralegal job. While he continued to send out résumés, he paid a visit to an employment agency which specialized in placing legal assistants in both temporary and permanent paralegal jobs. Although he lacked the paralegal education, the employment agency found him a temporary paralegal position in a major Wall Street law firm. One of the firm's clients was involved in antitrust litigation and there was a need to hire more nonlawyers to analyze the thousands of documents. The position would remain open indefinitely since it was uncertain if the case would be settled or go to trial.

Mitchell began to work at the law firm in November 1979 at the rate of $6.00 an hour. His salary was paid by the employment agency since the law firm had contracted through the agency for his services.

A few weeks later one of Mitchell's résumés resulted in an interview at another law firm in New York City. He was offered a job on the spot. When he told the Wall Street firm of this offer, he was offered the same salary as that offered by the other firm and a permanent job. He accepted this job offer since he enjoyed working at the firm. His salary was $210 a week.

As a temporary paralegal, he had not been given much background information about the antitrust case. As a permanent paralegal he was given three days' worth of files to read in order to familiarize himself with the case. At this point in the case, the firm had already gone through discovery of 27,000 documents.

For the first six weeks as a permanent paralegal he analyzed and summarized documents with the other ten paralegals hired to work on the case. The law firm had a team approach when working on a major case, and grouped paralegals and attorneys together to work on designated portions of the case. The other thirty-five paralegals in the firm worked on other litigation matters and in the real estate and corporate departments.

In addition to analyzing and summarizing documents, Mitchell also analyzed depositions, writing factual memoranda on the contracts, preparing exhibits for depositions, and attending depositions.

The work atmosphere was comfortable and informal, with everyone on a first-name basis. Mitchell shared an office with three other paralegals, had his own desk, phone extension, and his name on the door. Like the other paralegals he had the services of the stenography pool and duplicating department.

With a major case such as this one, paralegals did not have a regular nine to five work day. Mitchell frequently worked seventy hours a week. He worked regularly six days a week and sometimes on Sundays. He was paid overtime for this.

In January 1980 Mitchell and his team were sent to Los Angeles to take depositions for the case. His air transportation, accommodations, and meals were all "first class," but this was not a vacation; he worked around the clock. He assisted attorneys in preparing for the depositions and digested the deposition to transcripts as they were taken.

Upon his return from California, Mitchell had decided that he wanted to become an attorney. He was accepted at a national law school for the Fall of 1980. At law school he found that his paralegal training and work experience gave him a good foundation and introduction to law. Also, as a law student he found himself under pressure to complete assignments with deadlines; the work at the law firm had prepared him for this.

In October of his first year at law school he secured a position for the following summer as a first-year law associate at a small New York City law firm. Attaining a law job as a first-year law student is rare, and Mitchell attributed it to the fact that he had had nearly a year's experience working on a major litigation.

In his second year of law school Mitchell entered a writing competition for the *Urban Law Journal*. His writing abilities were judged to be excellent and he was made an editor on the *Journal*. After publishing a student article, he was selected to become the Editor-in-Chief of the law journal which gave him a full scholarship to pay for his last year of law school. He was given this honor based on his work performance on the journal, his management background from college, and his work experiences at the two law firms.

While a second-year law student, he also worked as a Federal Judicial Intern for a United States District Court Judge. With this experience and his private law firm experience Mitchell has been exposed to both the private law firm setting and the public law sector.

Mitchell feels that his career path was definitely influenced by his paralegal experience.

Medium-sized Law Firms

Medium-sized law firms of twenty to fifty-nine lawyers are also located in large metropolitan areas of the country. This type of practice will be very much like the larger firm's except that domestic and personal injury cases may be part of the firm's practice. Fewer paralegals will be employed in mid-sized than in large firms. They will usually have their own offices and may

Paralegals work closely with attorneys when assisting them in a legal matter.

share a secretary with only one other paralegal or an attorney.

These paralegals will usually be given more responsible and demanding assignments than in the larger firms. This will allow them to use on the job much of what they were taught in paralegal school. The paralegals will have more client contact, use more independent judgment, and be given more recognition in their work. The medium-sized firms usually allow their paralegals to perform legal research, write reports, and draft memoranda of law.

Profile—Working in a Medium-sized Law Firm

Margaret T. is a corporate paralegal working in a mid-sized Wall Street law firm. At age 40 she had grown dissatisfied with working as a volunteer in her town. With a bachelor's degree in education she decided to enroll in an intensive three-month legal assistant training program to become a litigation paralegal. After successfully completing the program in December 1980 she looked for a job.

She interviewed at four different law firms before she decided to accept the job offer at the firm where she is now employed. While seeking employment she worked in various temporary paralegal jobs through an employment agency to gain exposure to a variety of types of law firms. By the time she chose her paralegal position she was familiar with several kinds of paralegal jobs. She chose her present job because she would receive training in the field of corporate law, which would allow her to eventually work for a corporation if she chose to do so.

The law firm's philosophy was to train everyone, regardless of their previous background. Margaret was fortunate, however, since she had worked with municipal law through her volunteer work, so she started off with some practical legal experience.

She was hired at $15,000 per year to replace a corporate paralegal who was leaving the firm to begin work at a brokerage house. Her writing abilities were used right away. For the month that Margaret T. was being trained she was given very short Blue-Sky research assignments to complete. Her legal research classes were of great assistance to her since she had been given a memorandum of law to complete as part of the course. She was also taught by one of the senior associates how to use the blue sky reporters.

Two weeks after the other corporate paralegals had left, Margaret was working on her own. She began by working with senior associates but now usually works only for the firm's partner's.

Eight months after she began working at the firm she was given a raise of $1,250 and she is now negotiating for another salary review. Her benefits include four weeks paid vacation, life insurance, and full Blue Cross/Blue Shield coverage. When she works overtime, which is frequent in this high-pressured firm, she earns $13.25 per hour.

Once a month the corporate department has a luncheon for the attorneys and paralegals to discuss current matters the department is working on. Margaret's client contact is restricted to talking to clients on the telephone and meeting with them when they must sign papers.

After working a year in this firm Margaret T. has found that her work as a paralegal has been recognized and appreciated. She now is the head corporate paralegal with two paralegal assistants. Sometimes the lack of clear-cut administrative policies causes her concern since paralegals are sometimes treated differently from the attorneys.

However, she has interesting and challenging work as a paralegal. Her position allows her to hire other paralegals and delegate work to them. She has learned a lot from this job and would eventually like to use these skills she has acquired as a law firm administrator or as a paralegal working in a major corporation.

Small Law Firms and Sole Practitioners

The smaller general practice firm enables the paralegal to learn in depth about one or several types of law. This size law firm is usually located in a suburban or rural area. In a small office the paralegal can work on litigation, personal injury cases, criminal cases, bankruptcy proceedings, real estate transactions, and matrimonial cases. In the smaller office, the paralegal can be expected to perform receptionist and secretarial duties as well as paralegal work.

The paralegal who chooses to work in a small law firm will find that he/she is working closely both with the attorney and the clients. He/she will also find that he/she is expected to work with little direction from the attorney but at a high level of efficiency. Very often a paralegal working in this type of firm will be the only one employed.

The law library will probably not be as complete as the law libraries in larger firms. The paralegal will be expected to do legal research in the nearby bar association's law library. In addition, there may not be a secretary or other office staff to assist the paralegal. This means that very often the paralegal is responsible for typing and photocopying his/her own work.

One advantage to working in a small firm is being able to have extensive client contact. Much of the work delegated to the paralegal will be the same kind of work which a first-year associate would do in a bigger firm. Salaries may not be as high as those being paid to paralegals working in the larger firms, but the kind of training and experience received in the small firm will allow the legal assistant to become highly specialized in one or more areas of law.

Profile—Working for a Sole Practitioner

Vicki S., a paralegal working in Westchester County, New York, began her legal assistant career in 1975. An interior decorator in her mid-thirties, with a college degree in music, she sought a career change. She decided to attend a sixteen-week paralegal program in New York City and seek a legal assistant position in Westchester. Unable to get placement assistance from her paralegal program, and with very few paralegal positions available in Westchester County at that time, Vicki found that she had to invent an ingenious way to get "her foot in the door" in this career.

She was particularly interested in the area of family law and felt that her litigation specialty would stand her in good stead. She researched all of the matrimonial attorneys in Westchester County, chose the one with the busiest practice, and volunteered to work for him without pay during the summer to prove how valuable a paralegal could be to his practice.

Eager to try Vicki as a paralegal, the attorney spent many hours teaching her about his matrimonial practice. That summer her duties included filing and organizing files, interviewing some clients, and reading law journals to find relevant matrimonial cases which she digested on file cards for future reference. Later on in her paralegal career she found how valuable this experience was; it saved her much time when she was doing legal research on a particular case and wanted to refer back to relevant cases. She also added cases from advance sheets that came into the office.

By the end of July she was going to court with her employer. She discovered that the attorney was spending an hour and a half or more waiting for the judge to call a case, causing the attorney to lose time that he could be spending working at the office. At the $125 an hour he charged, Vicki figured out that he was losing about $250 each week. So she convinced him to allow her to go to court to answer calendar calls for him, and to call him to court, if necessary, to save him that $250. By the end of the summer, the attorney realized how indispensable Vicki had become to his practice, and arranged a part-time, two-day-a-week schedule for her at $40 a day. Her duties increased, and she attended examinations before trial, prepared orders to show causes and exhibits to be produced, and had more client contact.

Vicki found that her organizational abilities were the key to her success as the only paralegal working in this law office. A large desk calendar and a day-to-day diary became invaluable to her work. The diary would serve to remind her when and which papers were due into the office and court. She was then able to inform the clients so they could have the necessary papers ready on time. By becoming a notary she was able to notarize clients' signatures when needed.

Since the law practice was a busy one, Vicki found that she was meeting with many different clients each day. To refresh her memory before meeting with each client she would refer to the fact sheet she prepared for each one. She also knew that nothing could be sent out of the office without first being copied. This included all letters, checks, and legal documents.

One of Vicki's other major roles as a paralegal was to bring along a capsule summary of each case to prepare her to speak to the court clerks. Before going to court she made sure to find out how many copies were needed of each document and what the filing fees were.

The courts often proved to be slow when processing papers and Vicki found that anxious clients would want to know the reason for the delays in getting their case on the court calendar. To better accommodate the clients, Vicki asked to see how a certain type of paperwork was routed through the courts. She found that it would have to go through seven places before the card giving the date for the trial would arrive in the office. By being able to explain this to anxious clients, she was able to reassure them. Vicki's duties increased over the next few years to include drafting legal memoranda, writing motion papers and bills of particulars, and hiring the other personnel in the office. By 1980 she was making $100 a day.

Vicki proved to be a thorough, efficient, and professional matrimonial paralegal. After six-and-half years of working for one attorney, she decided that she would like to freelance as a matrimonial paralegal. She printed up new business cards, revised her résumé, and called up some of the attorneys she worked with through her firm's clients, and set her fee at $125 per day. In each law office she contracts with, she begins by reorganizing their files and ascertaining the papers needed to be served and answered. She draws up the client fact sheet and financial affidavit. Her client contact now includes four-way conferences with the husband, wife, and their attorneys.

Although she still works under the supervision of an attorney, she enjoys the independence of doing things her own way and controlling her own work schedule.

Corporations, Banks, and Insurance Companies

A paralegal employed by a corporation works in its legal department, one of the many departments in a large company. Such a job is like working in a small general practice law firm.

Some of the legal work that a corporation, bank, or insurance company is involved in will probably be done in conjunction with a law firm specializing in a certain kind of law, like litigation, real estate, or trusts and estates. It is very possible for a corporate paralegal to work for both the general counsel of a corporation and a law firm.

Paralegals find that working in a corporation allows them to have set working hours in contrast to a law firm's overtime hours, although a corporation will probably not offer the same variety of work as a law firm. Working conditions are not uniform in all companies, so before accepting a job, a paralegal should find out exactly what his/her duties will be.

Generally the corporate paralegal will work in the areas of securities, real estate, and state and federal incorporation regulations.

Benefits usually are excellent in a corporation, bank, or insurance company. Many offer reimbursements which allow the paralegal to continue his/her education in either law or business school. Secretarial help will be available as well as a well-equipped law library.

Corporate paralegals have a definite advantage in their jobs. As they become familiar with the company's operations in general, future job mobility within the company may become possible.

Profile—Working in an Insurance Company

After considerable study, a major insurance company based in Connecticut hired its first paralegal in 1975. Andrew L., a graduate of an associate degree paralegal program, was hired to work in the real estate investment department. He interviewed at five law firms before deciding to accept this job offer. He felt that insurance law would be a continually changing field and his employment possibilities would always remain excellent.

The insurance company now employs twenty-two paralegals, working in the areas of corporate, litigation, bond/investment, life insurance, and real estate/investment. In 1980 the company began its own formal paralegal program which allows for uniform standards in hiring, training, and promotion. The other twenty-one paralegals hired at an entry-level salary of $16,000 have been recruited from paralegal programs, other legal offices, and some are employees promoted from within the company.

Every two years the company takes a detailed look at their paralegal program to review its components. Surveys are sent to law firms and corporate legal departments to determine the relative importance of training and personality of the paralegal to job assignments. It also evaluates the importance of college education, in-house training, and trends in paralegal programs.

Andrew L. is considered to be part of the insurance company's technical, not administrative staff. He has a detailed matrix of job responsibilities and his own secretary. His health and insurance benefits are excellent but Andrew finds the educational benefits most important to his individual needs. Andrew finished his college education and is now attending law school in the evenings with the insurance company reimbursing him for all of his educational expenses.

The company is pleased with the contribution that Andrew L. and the other paralegals have made. To further their individual growth as paralegals, they are encouraged to join paralegal associations and attend seminars in the legal areas they are assigned to.

Profile—Paralegal Working in a Bank

After Carol B. graduated from college in 1966 with a bachelor's degree in history and political science, she worked for five years as a pension administrator for a major insurance company. When the department relocated to New Jersey, Carol, instead of joining the company, became involved in a local political organization.

By the time she was ready to resume her career in the field of employee benefits, she found that the ERISA law had made her prior knowledge of pension administration completely obsolete. It was at this point, in the summer of 1979, that she decided to enroll in a certificate paralegal's program. Since she was thinking of looking for a job in an insurance company or a bank after she completed the program, she chose the area of probate, estates, and trusts to major in. This specialization, along with her prior business background as a pension administrator, would allow her to reenter the job market with excellent credentials.

When she completed the three-month certificate program in August 1979 she mailed out over 200 résumés to law firms, banks, and insurance companies. While waiting for their replies, she went to an employment agency which specialized in placing legal assistants in temporary paralegal positions. The employment agency placed her in a law firm which soon began to train her as a litigation paralegal.

While working and being trained to become a litigation paralegal, Carol began to go for paralegal job interviews. Within six weeks she interviewed at several law firms and a bank. She chose the bank because she felt she would be offered the most opportunities to use both her paralegal training and her prior work background. The bank, located in a small nearby city, hired Carol at a salary of $12,500 and assigned her to the Trust Department. She was the second paralegal hired at the bank and the first trusts and estates paralegal. Carol was put on probation for six months, and at the end of that time she was given a good performance review and her salary was raised to $13,000 per year. After a year and a half she was making $15,400.

Carol's major job responsibilities are in the area of estate administration. She determines the estate's assets and values them according to the date-of-death values. She prepares inventories, listing assets held by the decedent at the date of death. She is also responsible for paying the bills for trust accounts.

She makes income projections for the estate on a monthly basis by examining all the stocks and bonds in accounts to determine the amount of dividends which will be coming in. She completes all the personal state and federal tax forms for the bank's clients and performs the accountings for estates and trusts.

As Carol became more capable, she was given larger, multi-million dollar estates to work on. The bank recognizes that she is clearly "officer material" and would like her to become a trust administrator or an assistant trust officer. It will send her for a special training session at the School of Banking at Williams College, and after a year of examinations she will graduate with a certificate enabling her to be promoted to an assistant trust officer or a trust administrator.

Without her specialized training in probate, estates, and trusts, Carol would never have made these advances in her career.

Profile—Working in a Major Corporation

Karen A., a Phi Beta Kappa graduate with a degree in history, graduated in 1962 and taught for a year before having her first child. After her child was born she returned to the teaching profession as a substitute teacher and continued to teach off and on for the next fifteen years while studying for her master's degree. She was never able to teach her specialty, history; she was always assigned to English or remedial reading classes, and as a result, she became dissatisfied with the education field.

She was contemplating a career change when she saw an advertisement in the newspaper for a paralegal training program. As a history major she had always had an interest in law but never considered going to law school since she had her four children in the years immediately following graduation from college.

Karen mentioned the possibility of attending a paralegal program to her husband, an attorney. Since he was familar with the paralegal as a valued assistant to an attorney he encouraged her to apply to a paralegal program.

Karen decided to attend a six-month certificate program which met in the evenings. This program concentrated on a general practice curriculum. This seemed to be the best kind of program for Karen to take since she lives in a somewhat rural area whose law firms have a general practice.

Before the end of the paralegal program Karen had secured

a position in a three-attorney general practice law firm. There were three secretaries for the three attorneys and Karen was their first paralegal. Her salary started at $12,000 a year, but she had no health or insurance benefits.

After working there for several months, Karen had an offer to interview at a Fortune 500 corporation's legal department. This interview was arranged by the paralegal program's placement office. Karen interviewed for the job and was offered it.

She decided to accept the job because there appeared to be more career advancement in working for a major corporation. The salary and benefits were better too, including full reimbursement for education expenses. Her salary jumped to $15,000 a year.

The legal department consists of eleven attorneys, seven secretaries, three paralegals, and one office manager. One of the paralegals is going to law school at night. The main areas that the legal staff concentrates in are securities law, litigation, real estate transactions, contract law, and tax law.

Karen performs some legal research and fact-finding. Her main job duties are concentrated on editing monthly operating reports, assisting in workman's compensation and personal injury cases, and digesting depositions. She has been sent to Washington, D.C. to assist in the discovery phase of a major litigation. At present, she is being trained in filing and renewing trademark registrations.

Although Karen feels that she is being given more and more responsible duties, she has not ruled out a job change from the legal department to another part of the corporation. She recently applied for a position as a marketing analyst which required some legal training.

Karen feels that paralegal training was essential for her to make the move from teaching to business. Without the certificate in paralegal studies, she believes that she would have had to study for a master's degree in business administration to have made the leap into the corporate setting without first being a secretary. Her understanding of business and the skills needed to succeed in it have given her the opportunity to begin a second career.

Court Administration

The court system offers numerous opportunities for paralegals to work in legal and quasi-legal positions. Some of these job titles will not be "Paralegal" or "Legal Assistant" necessarily, but the job descriptions will describe a position which utilizes paralegal training. The court system uses a variety of personnel who must have prior legal training or legally related experience. Examples of these positions are court assistants, court clerks, investigators, adjustors, trial specialists, and surrogate court assistants. The best way to find out about these positions is to visit the county personnel office and check the postings on its bulletin boards. A court assistant starts at a salary of $16,700 per year. A court clerk's entry-level salary is $18,600.

Profile—Court Administrator

Marion D. worked as a court assistant in the Civil Division of the Supreme Court, Westchester County, New York State, Ninth Judicial District, for four years before she attended an evening general practice certificate paralegal program. Without a college degree, she knew that she would have to attain additional education in order to qualify for a higher level position in the courthouse.

In her job as a court assistant, she assisted in the court's various procedures. She typed court calendars, kept index books and index cards up-to-date with notes of issues, and sent post cards to attorneys notifying them of the date a particular case would be put on the calendar for the first time.

In 1979 when she completed the paralegal program she took the examination for the court clerk position. As part of her training she worked in the County Clerk's Office for about six months in the criminal, accident, and civil Parts. Her position now is in the Supreme Court's contested matrimonial actions where there are trials and motions. The matrimonial part is divided between contested and uncontested divorces. There are two other clerks in addition to Marion working in the matrimonial part. The other two work in uncontested divorces and hearings.

Marion's job entails being able to work well with the public. She deals on a daily basis with judges, attorneys, and their clients.

She must also be competent in her work. She must know what to check for when papers are delivered by the attorneys. Without an index number or an affidavit of service, there can be numerous delays and problems in a case.

She also types the calendars for trials and motions, reads the decisions from the judges, and marks in a book the date that a decision was rendered, and whether the matter was to be resolved or stricken.

Much of Marion's work also involves going into the courtroom. During a trial she might take minutes, handle exhibits, and swear in jurors and witnesses.

Marion is now completing her associate degree in liberal arts. She found her paralegal training to be useful in understanding some of the legal theory and procedures which are behind the matrimonial cases in her job. With this type of knowledge and her varied and extensive experience working in the courthouse, she may eventually apply to become an assistant to the Chief Court Clerk.

Government

The government is a major employer of paralegals. Paralegals are working in all levels—federal, state, county, and city. These positions require that applicants take an examination and be put on a list to await a permanent appointment. Notices for these examinations are posted in government office buildings, or you can pay a visit to an agency's personnel office for more information. There are also specific educational and/or experiential requirements which must be met. Some provisional appointments may be made, however, when the agency is waiting for the examination to be given again but needs to hire people to fill an immediate need.

In the federal government paralegals are employed as legal technicians and paralegal specialists. To be considered for these jobs, you must take the Professional and Administrative Career Examination (PACE). A legal technician may type, monitor cases, set up files, and draft form pleadings. He/she must have a knowledge of legal documents and processes. A paralegal specialist assists attorneys in litigation, monitors discovery documents, drafts legal memoranda, and interviews witnesses.

The following information is from the United States Office of Personnel Management, Standards Development Center, Washington, D. C. 20415. These descriptions of job duties are part of a draft of proposed classification and Qualification Standards for the Paralegal Series, GS-0950 (1981).

Paralegal Specialist, GS-5

Duties. A trainee paralegal is assigned a variety of duties intended to provide the employee with a good working knowledge of agency programs, policy, regulations, and implementing legislation. In this capacity, the employee:

- Consults prescribed sources of information for facts relating to matters of interest to the program;
- Reviews subpoenaed documents to extract selected data and information relating to specified items;
- Summarizes information in prescribed format on case precedents and decisions;

- Searches for legal references in libraries and by means of computer data banks;
- Accompanies attorneys to hearings and court appearances to assist in the presentation of charts and other visual information and to become informed on court procedures and the status of cases.

Paralegal Specialist, GS-7

Duties. In a developmental capacity the employee serves as a paralegal providing legal assistance to attorneys. In this capacity he/she:

- Reviews case materials to become familiar with questions under consideration;
- Searches for and summarizes relevant articles in trade magazines, law reviews, published studies, financial reports, and similar materials;
- Prepares summaries of research findings for use of attorneys in the preparation of opinions, briefs, and other legal documents;
- Interviews potential witnesses, and prepares summary interview reports for the attorney;
- Participates in pretrial witness conferences, notes any deficiencies in case materials and additional matters requiring investigation prior to trial, and requests further investigation by other agency personnel to correct deficiencies;
- Prepares and organizes trial exhibits, such as statistical charts and photographic exhibits;
- Verifies citations and legal references on prepared legal documents;
- Prepares summaries of testimony and depositions;
- Drafts and edits nonlegal memoranda, research reports, and correspondence relating to cases.

Most of the positions in the legal clerk and legal technician series require the employee to perform one or more clerical functions, such as:

- Initiating and composing standardized legal forms routinely needed for specific legal actions;
- Accepting service of legal documents, reviewing for correct

form and timeliness, annotating case files and status records
to reflect receipt and due date for response or other actions
required;
· Maintaining docket calendars and tickler systems, coordi-
nating schedules with clerks of courts, reminding attorneys
of court appearances and deadlines for submitting various
actions or documents, notifying witnesses of appearances
and of changes resulting from suspensions or settlements;
· Establishing, maintaining, and closing out case files or
systems of legal records, annotating indices and status
records, compiling workload and status reports, and locating
and abstracting data from files and records.

Attorney General's Office

In a state's attorney general's office, the paralegals may be
assigned to either the criminal or civil division.

The attorney general (state's attorney) represents the public
and the state in cases involving consumer protection, tenants
and homeowners, energy and utility services, environmental
protection, civil rights, protection of workers, protection of in-
vestors, regulation of charities and trusts, and criminal investigations and prosecutions. This office defends the state's laws and
public policies, represents state agencies and officials in prisoner-
related litigation, claims and collections, and in taxation and
revenue issues.

Legal assistants working in the attorney general's office can be
assigned a variety of job duties. In the litigation bureau they
may assist in the preparation of motions, pleadings, briefs, trials,
and appellate records. In the antitrust bureau they may assist
in document work and participate in investigations of possible
violations of the criminal and civil provisions of the antitrust
laws.

In the consumer frauds and protection bureau they may assist
the attorneys in investigating complaints regarding possible
violations of consumer protection statutes and in preparing for
a consumer frauds litigation.

In the real estate financing bureau of the attorney general's
office legal assistants may explain the legal aspects of cooperative
and condominium conversions to the public, elected officials, and
tenants. They may assist in regulating the workload of attorneys
in the investigation and prosecution of real estate fraud.

In the investor protection and securities bureau paralegals

may assist in the review of broker–dealer and salesmen statements, takeover registration statements, and theatrical and franchise prospectus submissions.

In the charities, trusts, and estates bureau paralegals may assist attorneys in the investigation and litigation of cases involving hospitals.

Although a college degree is not mandatory, a paralegal certificate from an accredited paralegal assistant training program is required for a legal assistant position with an attorney general's office. Entry-level salaries range from $13,000 to $15,000. Vacation, health, and insurance benefits are good.

Since this is a civil service position, legal assistants working in this office must eventually take an examination. Provisional appointments are made before an examination is passed.

Available legal assistant positions may be posted in state office buildings or advertised in newspapers.

There may be on-the-job training available in some states. For example, the New York State Department of Law is starting a "Bridge Program" whereby it will move clerical staff into legal assistant positions after they have worked for two years in the office. This program will be supplemented by outside paralegal courses.

Some of the New York state agencies where paralegals are utilized are in the Department of Social Services, Department of Health Services, and Department of Transportation. The job duties for these agencies include similar responsibilities as those in the Attorney General's Office. In general, such paralegals may perform legal research, assist in trial preparation, control documents, and docket cases. They may administer crime victim programs, assist in civil rights actions, and serve as consumer fraud representatives. They may draft complaints, accusations, statements of issue, interview witnesses, attend depositions, digest depositions, maintain files on legislative and regulatory issues, organize documents, and do investigative work.

Paralegals are also used in county and city governments by the district attorney's office, county public defender's office, and the city attorney's office.

District Attorney's Office

The district attorney's office (also referred to as the county attorney's office in some states) is the county office which

Many paralegals have assignments which bring them into the courthouse.

represents the state in criminal prosecutions. The funding for this office is derived from the federal, state, and city governments.

The types of cases referred to the district attorney's office are those involving domestic violence, child abuse, juvenile offenses, homicides, fraud, and other major offenses.

A paralegal is considered to be an integral part of this office, and he/she works both independently and as a member of a team.

Paralegals screen cases with the district attorney, assist in writing up the cases, perform legal research, help to manage special bureaus, and accompany assistant district attorneys on homicide calls.

To apply for a position in a district attorney's office a paralegal graduate must submit a résumé to the D.A. and interview with the personnel office. When there is an opening in the office, and provided that the paralegal "passed" the interview, he/she can join the office. There is a special test which is given to paralegals after they have worked about a year.

There are standard health and insurance benefits, and between two and three weeks paid vacation the first year of employment.

The work day is usually 9 A.M. to 5 P.M. Entry-level salaries for paralegals are in the range of $12,700. There are also opportunities to gain supervisory experience.

City Government

City governments are often major employers of paralegals. If you live in a major city and are interested in working in the public sector, city government can offer excellent employment opportunities. The primary areas where a paralegal may work in the city attorney's office are in torts, general litigation, and commercial litigation. New York City, for example, has 140 nonlawyers assisting the 500 attorneys on the staff of the New York City Office of the Corporation Counsel.

The Corporation Counsel employs paralegal aides, claim examiners, investigators, and principal administrative associates. All of these positions require some knowledge or experience working in law.

Salary ranges for these jobs are from $12,500 to $23,000 depending on the title and your experience. Generally there is an 8 percent raise per year. Merit raises can add an additional 7 percent to salaries.

These employees have their own secretarial support staff, some with word-processing equipment.

The following information is from the New York City Corporation Counsel's office. The job descriptions are for paralegal aide, claim examiner, and investigator.

Paralegal Aide—General Statement of Duties and Responsibilities. Under supervision, with latitude for the exercise of independent initiative and judgment, performs a variety of paralegal duties; performs related work.

Examples of Typical Tasks: Interviews clients, witnesses, victims, and complainants; assists in the preparation and service of legal papers, e.g., motions, subpoenas, and other documents; performs legal research; collects, assembles, and assists in evaluating evidence and technical data for use in trials and proceedings; prepares witnesses and arranges for appearance of witnesses at trials; maintains court calendars and schedules; may conduct investigations, examine and adjust claims, and conduct closings on real estate titles and mortgages; may be responsible for the overall management of caseload; monitors case flow and movement; maintains control of all relevant information for the prosecution of a case; may collect and analyze data to determine the effectiveness of programs; monitors compliance with federal and state guidelines for grant projects; prepares analyses of testimony; summarizes briefs and court decisions; prepares reports on individual cases or groups of cases; assists in all forms of legal proceedings, programs and projects.

Qualification Requirements

1. Completion of an acceptable course of study at a school preparing individuals for service as paralegal aides, legal assistants, or similar title; or
2. An associate degree or completion of 60 credits from an accredited college; or
3. High school graduation or evidence of having passed an examination for the high school equivalency diploma, *and* three years of full-time paid acceptable paralegal experience in a governmental, public, or private law office or legal department, or in the court system; or
4. A satisfactory equivalent.

Experience as a legal secretary, clerk, investigator, or in other fields where duties are not of a paralegal nature will not be acceptable toward meeting the minimum requirements.

Claim Examiner—General Statement of Duties and Responsibilities. Under direct supervision, investigates personal injury, property damage, and miscellaneous claims against the City or public authority and affirmative claims of the City or authority against others; performs related work.

Examples of Typical Tasks: Investigates and assists in the preparation for trial of less serious claims against the City; secures evidence by interviewing interested parties, witnesses, doctors, and other persons involved; makes physical inspections of accident scenes; obtains relevant documents, records, maps, exhibits, photographs, etc., and such information from records of public agencies and private organizations as may be pertinent. Submits all such information in the form of a written report; arranges for court appearances, through subpoena or otherwise, of witnesses required for proper presentation of a case; confers with the attorney assigned to a case regarding the facts developed during investigation, and otherwise assists the attorney before and during trial; interprets rules and regulations as applied to minor claims; may make recommendations as to approval or disallowance of such claims, for example refunds and miscellaneous law claims; prepares the court calendars and attends court calendar calls.

Qualification Requirements

1. Graduation from a senior high school and three (3) years of satisfactory, full-time, paid experience in investigating or adjusting liability claims for a railroad or other transportation company, insurance company, governmental agency, or law office; or
2. A baccalaureate degree issued after completion of a four-year course in an accredited college or university; or
3. A satisfactory equivalent.

Investigator—General Statement of Duties and Responsibilities. Under supervision, makes investigations designed to prevent or detect violations of laws relating to tax liabilities and delinquencies, or violations of miscellaneous rules and regulations of the various municipal administrative agencies, or makes investigations designed to determine qualifications for civil service employment; performs related work.

Examples of Typical Tasks: Obtains information regarding liability of delinquent taxpayers; investigates corporations and organizations soliciting funds from the public; makes searches in depositories of public and private records to determine financial standing of tax debtors; apprehends violators of laws governing solicitation of funds from public, causes arrests, signs complaints, makes physical inspections and diagrams at scenes of accidents; locates and interviews prospective witnesses in actions in which the City of New York or its agencies are defendants, conducts examinations under oath and serves legal process; assembles and verifies data pertinent to settlement or adjudication of tort claims; conducts investigations in hospitals and other institutions to determine eligibility of patients for care at public expense; verifies information concerning education, experience, and other personal qualifications bearing upon character and fitness of applicants for employment in the municipal civil service; examines and analyzes records and documents; reports on results of personal interviews or interrogation of witnesses; testifies at hearings and in court proceedings.

Qualification Requirements. Graduation from a senior high school, or possession of a high school equivalency diploma, or an equivalent G.E.D. certificate issued by the Armed Forces, and

1. Four (4) years of satisfactory, full-time, paid experience as an investigator, of which two (2) years must have been as an investigator in the field; or
2. A baccalaureate degree issued after completion of a four-year course of study in an accredited college or university; or
3. A satisfactory equivalent.

The Nonprofit Sector

Positions for trained paralegals in the public interest sector are very often dependent on funding by the government or by foundation grants.

American Civil Liberties Union

The American Civil Liberties Union is an example of an agency employing paralegals which is supported by foundation grants and private donations. The national headquarters is located in New York City. There are affiliate organizations located throughout the United States. The larger affiliates and the national headquarters employ paralegals. Some of the larger affiliates are located in California, Michigan, New Jersey, Ohio, and Texas.

This organization deals with issues that relate to civil liberties as set out in the United States Constitution. Some examples of the kinds of cases that the ACLU may become involved in against the government and its agencies include sex discrimination, abortion, separation of church and state, children's rights, alien rights, and pornography. These cases are often controversial in nature. The paralegal's job involves continual contact with attorneys and the public.

Informational interviewing and making referrals to other private agencies are other aspects of an ACLU paralegal's job.

Specific job duties of these paralegals include performing factual research and investigative work. Their pretrial and trial work includes digesting depositions and assisting the attorneys in the courtroom by compiling data and charting statistical information. Many of these paralegals work on legislative projects: They attend legislative hearings to collect information.

The entry-level salary for a paralegal working in this agency is $17,500. Although there is no overtime paid to the paralegals, they are given four weeks paid vacation and health and insurance benefits. Salary increases are granted on a yearly basis. To apply for a paralegal job in the ACLU, a résumé should be sent to the office manager.

For further information regarding the American Civil Liberties Union write to its headquarters:

American Civil Liberties Union
National Headquarters
132 West 43 Street
New York, NY 10036

Legal Aid Societies

A Legal Aid Society employs paralegals in the civil and criminal divisions. The criminal division represents clients accused of murder, rape, burglary, robbery, serious assaults, and child abuse. The civil division handles landlord–tenant, consumer credit, Social Security, Medicaid, and divorce cases. The funding for these organizations comes from county and state governments with some appropriations from the federal government. Legal Services Corporation funds 30 percent of the civil division of the Legal Aid Society and determines the eligibility guidelines for the Society's clients. In addition, major corporations may make donations.

A paralegal working in a Legal Aid Society may write and serve subpoenas, submit reports on the results of an investigation, serve orders and have them certified, interview clients who are incarcerated, and testify in the courtroom on behalf of clients.

The chief counsel who heads the agency is responsible for the hiring of paralegals. A typical entry-level salary for a paralegal ranges from between $10,000 to $14,000 per year.

Legal Services Corporation

The Legal Services Corporation is a federal independent agency which provides funding to legal services groups nationwide, representing the urban and rural poor. This corporation which began in 1974 employs attorneys, paralegals, intake officers, community workers, and secretaries who provide legal services to these economically disadvantaged. Its headquarters is in Washington, D. C. Its board of directors is comprised of individuals employed in various segments of the legal community.

The Legal Services Corporation has offices in every state of the union and in Puerto Rico. Many of these offices employ paralegals as members of their staffs. These offices are considered to be "community-based" since they are located in the neighborhoods of many of their clients.

The paralegals who work in this corporation are employed to assist attorneys in areas of law which affect individuals: welfare, employment, housing, and immigration. The clients who cannot afford basic civil legal services include single mothers, homeless families, immigrant families, victims of consumer fraud, the elderly, and the handicapped. Legal Services also assists tenants, workers, and people who have been discriminated against in employment, housing, or other matters.

In the local offices, paralegals, under the direction of lawyers, assist Legal Services clients by interviewing them; opening case files when the client has been determined to have a legitimate claim; instructing the client on what to bring to an administrative hearing; preparing clients and witnesses for direct testimony; and representing the client at an administrative hearing and to an appeals board. The paralegal on occasion will perform questioning and cross-examining. He/she may also write and submit legal memoranda to the hearing officer. Of course only the attorney can bring a court action on behalf of the client.

In addition to the Legal Services Corporation's local offices, there are the national support centers which also employ paralegals. These centers specialize in a single area of law: women and family law, employment law, welfare law, immigration law, or consumer law. The centers will provide assistance to the local offices when they are asked. For instance, in a complex case, the support centers may assist in discovery work or order documents and evidence.

Each of the national support centers deals with all of the issues that confront its clients. The women and family law center, for example, handles cases involving divorce, custody, child support, termination of parental rights, domestic violence, and child abuse.

Many Legal Services employees have organized into unions. The National Association of Legal Services Workers is now affiliated with District 65 of the United Auto Workers (UAW). Its members include lawyers, paralegals, secretaries, intake officers, and social workers.

Local offices also act as referral centers for legal problems the office is unable to assist in, such as criminal cases. It is also involved in community training programs to educate administrative agencies and the public.

The entry-level salary for a paralegal varies as to the part of the country. It ranges usually from $12,000 to $18,000 a year dependent on the paralegal's background. Benefits also vary.

A college degree and paralegal training is helpful in obtaining a position with organizations funded by the Legal Services Corporation. Good communication skills are stressed since paralegals have a great deal of client contact and are also requested to write legal memoranda. Speaking a second language in addition to English can also be of assistance in the job. Most importantly, however, is the paralegal's commitment to the clients. The paralegal must be aggressive in representing them.

4. Type of Work According to Specialization

Paralegal training will familiarize you with one or several areas of law. After you receive formal paralegal training, you must be open to also learning on the job. The formalized training only gives you a foundation of knowledge. You must continually build on this knowledge through on-the-job training and continuing paralegal education.

The following text outlines some of the job duties you can expect as a working paralegal under the supervision of an attorney.

Litigation

As a paralegal working in the litigation area you will be responsible for organizing and managing documents for civil or criminal trials. Because some cases are more complex than others, it is important that a paralegal responsible for managing the case documents be aware of all the phases of litigation. A paralegal working in litigation might be responsible for organizing and preparing pleadings, case outlines, manuals for complex litigation, discovery requests, and interrogatories. He/she may digest depositions, index documents, operate computers, and draft pretrial and posttrial memoranda.

Some litigation paralegals perform the initial client interviews, gather the information about witnesses, compile medical information, prepare exhibits for use as evidence at trial, and serve subpoenas.

Litigation paralegals may draft pleadings, answer interrogatories, answer motions, and prepare factual analyses.

There are often deadlines to meet in litigation so a person choosing to work in this area must be able to remain cool in pressure situations.

Personal Injury Litigation

Personal injury litigation involves tort law. A paralegal working in this type of litigation would be involved in negligence, professional malpractice, and products liability. This type of work is a branch of civil litigation.

Corporations and Securities

Paralegals working in corporations and securities law will be actively involved in assisting in the formation, continuation, and dissolution of corporations. They may draft the following documents: Powers of attorney, promissory notes, bills of sales, transfers of assets, corporate tax returns, and stock transfers.

They may draft and file proxy statements under the Exchange Act of 1934—8-K forms, 9-K forms, 10-Q forms, and 10-K forms.

In the Blue Sky (state security laws) area these paralegals may draft and file applications for broker–dealers, investment advisors, and salesmen, compile exhibits for applications, and draft and file notices of exemption.

They may be expected to maintain a file of forms: Blue Sky, annual reports, foreign qualifications, and UCC.

A corporations and securities paralegal must be capable of doing detailed work, keeping accurate records, and interacting well with business people, paralegals, and lawyers.

Probate, Trusts, and Estates

Trusts and estates paralegals assist in the preparation of the legal documents associated with estate planning. They can participate in the collection of assets, maintenance of records, and notification of beneficiaries.

They are able to complete tax returns for the state and federal governments, prepare accounting records, file tax waivers, and draft closing documents.

These paralegals should have good mathematical abilities and enjoy interacting with clients.

Real Estate

Real estate paralegals draft most documents associated with purchases and sales of property. Some of these documents may be deeds, trust agreements, estoppel certificates, partnership and joint venture agreements, regulatory agreements, and security agreements.

Title work is very often delegated to paralegals. They are expected to do title searches, prepare abstracts, draft title opinions, and complete title insurance forms.

Many real estate paralegals draft escrow papers and open escrow accounts.

In tax matters they are often expected to compute taxes, draft and file abatements of taxes, file appeals with the Appellate Tax Board, attend tax board hearings, and draft and file tax injunctions.

With the increase of condominium and cooperative ownership, paralegals are trained to draft presentations and exhibits, set up closing procedures, arrange for title certification, and compile postclosing files.

Some real estate paralegals research issues involving environmental law, urban law, and recent legislature involving real estate and tax laws.

Real estate paralegals must have the ability to work well under pressure, and enjoy doing research.

Employee Benefits

Paralegals working in employee benefits law will assist attorneys in the drafting of pension and profit-sharing plans, including their design, installation, and administration. They may also aid in the design of deferred compensation plans, stock option plans, and health and medical plans.

They assist in the preparation of the filings required by the Internal Revenue Service for the qualification of employee benefit plans.

These paralegals must be able to understand the tax mathematics of the design of employee benefit plans, have an aptitude for working with figures and numbers, have the ability of securing information from clients, and have good writing skills.

Commercial Bankruptcy

Paralegals working in commercial bankruptcy will assist in drafting and filing Uniform Commercial Code financing statements, perform administrative work with creditors' committees, analyze financing statements, prepare routine bankruptcy pleadings, maintain bankruptcy dockets, and perform some legal research. The legal research entailed may involve researching financing statement filing requirements, classification of debts and creditors, and classification of collateral and available remedies.

Family Law

Paralegals working in family law conduct initial client interviews. They often draft adoption petitions, separation agreements, and divorce petitions.

The paralegal will have to know about community property systems, parent–child duties and responsibilities, paternity, adoption, juvenile delinquency, and legitimation proceedings. Much of family law is involved in litigation proceedings, so the paralegal will be required to work in litigation as well.

Administrative Law

Paralegals working in administrative law will apply and research relevant statutory and regulatory provisions at the federal and state levels, draft proposed rules and regulations, and assist in the preparation for administrative law hearings. These paralegals can make preliminary drafts of documents, briefs, and opinions. They are also able to assist attorneys at the appellate stage of an administrative law proceeding.

Employment Outlook for New Specializations

For the paralegal interested in making a long-term commitment to the legal field, it is essential to explore new law specializations. He/she can gain expertise in these areas through paralegal training programs, continuing education seminars, and on-the-job training.

The following are a few areas of law which will be increasing their utilization of paralegals.

Probate, Estates, and Trusts Law (Areas Affected by the Economic Recovery Tax Act of 1981)

Paralegals working in a probate practice can become further specialized in the field by studying the significance of fiduciary income-tax planning. This also includes postmortem estate planning and estate planning.

Commerical Real Estate

Paralegals working in commercial real estate will assist attorneys in planning creative financing approaches, condominium and cooperative conversions, and the tax consequences of real estate transactions.

Complex Litigation (Computers and Litigation Support)

Paralegals working in complex litigation cases will assist in the administration of complex cases through the application of computer technology and management of documents.

Oil and Gas Law

Paralegals working in oil and gas will render direct assistance to lawyers, the courts, and clients in compliance with state and federal gas laws.

Paralegals will assist in the preparing and drafting of oil and gas leases (for example, the granting clause, habendum clause, pooling clause, royalty clause, drilling, delay rental clause, and covenants implied in oil and gas leases).

They will also work under the supervision of an attorney in reviewing and drafting division orders, researching issues relating to oil and gas laws, and searching title records to prove ownership and transfer of title.

5. Finding Employment as a Paralegal

Securing your first job as a paralegal will be fairly easy if you have graduated from a reputable paralegal program in your geographic area.

The good news about looking for a paralegal position is that jobs are always becoming available. A paralegal usually stays in his/her first position for two years before moving on to another job, or going on to law school or business school, or being promoted to an administrative or managerial position in his/her firm or company. Whenever an employed paralegal makes a job change, another paralegal position opens up. In addition, new positions are continually being created as lawyers realize the economic advantages in using paralegals in their practices.

The best way to guarantee yourself a paralegal position as quickly as possible is to take an *active approach* in seeking it. The active approach to job seeking means hitting every angle when you are looking for your paralegal job. Only about 20 percent of the available jobs are advertised. The other 80 percent are found by remembering that looking for a job is a full-time job in itself.

When you start to look for a job tell all your friends and acquaintances that you are looking for a paralegal position. Read the newspapers and their classified advertisements for paralegal jobs, and most importantly, send out your résumé to law firms, corporations, banks, insurance companies, public agencies—any place that might hire a paralegal.

Writing the Résumé

Personal marketing is seventy percent of finding a job. Only thirty percent depends on actual background and skills. That personal marketing is in the form of a well-written résumé and good interviewing skills. Your first marketing tool is your résumé. Plan your résumé around the following: Your abilities, skills, and talents; what direction you want to take in your career;

what type of firm, corporation, or public agency you want to work for; and your interests.

Take an inventory of your skills. Write out a list of your accomplishments, no matter how insignificant they may seem to you. Examples could be: getting a driver's license, working your way through college, raising six children. Then select several accomplishments and write a paragraph or two about each one. State what you did, why you did it, how you did it, and what resulted from your activities. Then get someone to help you identify the skills you used to accomplish the tasks. You will then begin to realize the extent of your skills. Recognizing these skills will make you feel more comfortable in your job search.

Your résumé is your sales brochure and you are the product. Your résumé should reflect your skills and talents but it won't get you the job. It will introduce you to prospective employers and get you an interview but it will not get you a job.

Your résumé is your basic selling tool. It is a representation of yourself. Without a well-written résumé a prospective employer will not even consider you for an interview. Your résumé for the legal community will probably not differ too much from a résumé for the general business community. The most important adjective to remember when writing this résumé is "conservative." The résumé should be reproduced on white or cream-colored paper with at least a 25 percent rag content. And every résumé sent out must be accompanied by an individually typed cover letter on the same kind of paper that the résumé was copied on. If possible, use a matching legal-sized envelope. It may seem unnecessary but remember that this is the employer's first impression of you. It is important that this first impression be a good one so that he/she will be sufficiently interested and impressed to ask you in for an interview.

As mentioned before, your résumé is your marketing tool used to elicit the interview. Depending on your experience and background you may choose one of the following résumé formats: the reverse chronological approach or the functional approach. Since the paralegal profession attracts people with all kinds of experience and backgrounds, I suggest these two different approaches to résumé-writing based on the paralegal's existing experiences. The reverse chronological approach is simply an historical review of your work experience and educational background with the most recent listed first. Dates should be included in this type of résumé. Usually, recent college graduates will put their educational background first, under the heading of "Education." The first school to be mentioned should be the paralegal school that you attended, with a listing of the courses or areas of legal study that were offered. Some paralegal programs may offer bachelors' or associate degrees in paralegal studies. Remember to clearly emphasize the areas of study included in this paralegal program as well. Your internship experience, if any, can be included here, too. Leave room to add any academic distinctions if the résumé is prepared prior to graduation. Employers are impressed by better-than-average grades.

If you have graduate level courses in a field unrelated to the legal field you may include that information as well. Many interviewers seek out students with some postbaccalaureate courses.

And last in the reverse chronogical list of your educational background should be your undergraduate institution, with your major and minor areas of study. Any honors received should also be included. High school is included if you have not taken any college courses.

Unless your work experience is relevant to finding a position as a legal assistant, you should put your educational history first. This is the area which will be most attractive to the interviewer since the paralegal program you graduated from will be listed first.

Your work experience follows your educational background in this type of résumé. You may think that the jobs you held in order to put yourself through college or the jobs unrelated to the legal profession are not important to the employer. This is not so. Lawyers and legal administrators are very interested in noting longevity on a job or the fact that you put yourself through college. So include this information. Include a description of your job duties. Responsibilities such as interacting with the public, performing research, and writing reports are skills that can be transferred to the paralegal profession. Remember, too, that you must list these jobs in reverse chronological order.

I sometimes recommend to paralegals that "Hobbies" or "Special Interests" be included on the résumé. I suggest this either when the résumé looks a bit skimpy because the paralegal has had very little work history or because by including some personal facts, the paralegal will have an easier time interviewing. More than just a few paralegals have secured positions based in part on the fact that they had a hobby in common with the interviewer!

At the bottom of the résumé page you should include the statement "References Furnished Upon Request." This signals the conclusion of the résumé. I suggest you prepare a separate sheet of paper listing your references by name, title, address, and phone number. This should be photocopied so that during the interview, if and when you are asked for the names of references, you can present the interviewer with this list of references, instead of wasting time thumbing through an address or telephone book. You will appear more professional by doing so. Of course, you will always ask your references for permission to use their names.

Some paralegals put a job objective on their résumé. This is not necessary and is totally up to the paralegal. An objective simply is a statement of the kind of position you are seeking. Unless your objective is general in scope, it can narrow your job search. If you are willing to relocate or travel, however, you should include that information. This can either be put into a synopsis or in a category labeled "Of Special Interest" toward the end of your résumé.

I also recommend the functional approach résumé. In this kind of résumé you need not put any dates, names of employers, or job descriptions. This résumé basically highlights a person's experiences and groups skills together, and analyzes and draws out the traits common to them. For example, a graduate of a paralegal certificate program might have worked as a teacher and a social worker before he/she decided to change careers. The educational history would be listed in the same fashion as it would be in the reverse chronological résumé but only the job titles would be listed. A separate category entitled "Analysis of Experience" would follow. This category would analyze the skills used in the jobs of teaching and social work. Possible categories could include: administrative skills, interpersonal skills, counseling skills, and writing skills. These skills are emphasized since they are applicable to skills used when performing paralegal duties.

Once your résumé is letter-perfect it is ready to be reproduced by offset. You must decide how much you are willing to invest in these résumés and your job search. I feel that the cost of making copies of the résumé is negligible when you consider all of the doors that will open for you in your new career as a result of a professional-looking résumé.

Now study the model résumés that follow.

Sample Résumé for a Person with Extensive Work History (Functional Approach)

```
Name
Address
City, State, Zip Code
Area Code/Phone Number
```

OBJECTIVE   College graduate seeks position utilizing
                     paralegal training. Can offer variety of skills
                     combining intensive legal training and strong
                     administrative experience.

EDUCATION

  5/83   XYZ Certificate Paralegal Program, City State.
                     Intensive 200-hour course with training in the
                     following areas: Probate, Estates, and Trusts;
                     Litigation; Legal Research; Real Estate;
                     Matrimonial and Criminal Law. Special interests
                     in business organizations, client interviews and
                     case preparation.

  12/82   State University of New York at Albany.
                     M.A. Political Science

  6/66   Hunter College, New York, New York.
                     B.A. in Political Science
                     Minor in Sociology
                        Honors: Dean's List

EXPERIENCE
                     Teacher, White Plains, New York.
                     Administrative Assistant, New York, N.Y.

                     Executive Member of the Chappaqua Homeowners
                     Association; special liaison and spokesperson
                     between the Town Board of Chappaqua and the area
                     residents.

                     Founding Member of League of Women Voters in
                     community.

                     Active member of local political organization.

ANALYSIS OF EXPERIENCE

  Administrative: Organizing data; maintaining records; managing
                     files; planning skills.

  Research: Abstracting and synthesizing ideas; strong
                     writing skills; evaluation skills.

  Interpersonal: Effective interfacing; strong oral presentation
                     skills; group leadership abilities.

REFERENCES
                     Furnished upon request.

Sample Résumé for a Graduate of a Four-Year or Two-Year Paralegal Program

Name
Address
City, State, Zip Code
Area Code/Phone Number

EMPLOYMENT OBJECTIVE: I seek a challenging opportunity as a
                          paralegal.

EDUCATION:

September, 1979 -   XYZ College, City, State.
May, 1983   B.S. in Paralegal Studies
                          Cumulative Grade Point Average - 3.8
                          Departmental Honors. Dean's List.

WORK EXPERIENCE:

Summer, 1982   Camp Fernwood, Cedarhurst, N.Y.
                         Camp Counselor. Supervised group of
                         ten-year-old girls.

June 1981 -   Chatham Golf Club, Harrison, N.Y.
May, 1982   Administrative Assistant. Handled diverse
                         responsibilities: organizing and maintaining
                         filing system, monthly membership billing, club
                         correspondence.

Summer, 1980   Camp Inwood, Oxford, Maine.
                         Camp Counselor. Supervised group of
                         eight-year-old girls.

Summer, 1979   Lane Temporary Services, New York, N.Y.
                         Various clerical and secretarial positions.

EXTRACURRICULAR
ACTIVITIES:
                         Student Court Justice (1979-1983)
                         Student Congress Representative (1978-1979)
                         Member of Delta Phi Zeta, Social Services
                           Sorority (1980-1983)
                         Intramural Sports (1979-1983)

REFERENCES:
                         Furnished upon request.

Sample Résumé for a College Graduate with a Certificate in Paralegal Studies (Reverse Chronological)

```
Name
Address
City, State, Zip Code
Area Code/Phone Number
```

OBJECTIVE: Seeking a challenging position as a paralegal. Able to offer specialized training in Litigation, Trial Preparation, and Legal Research. Willing to travel and/or relocate.

EDUCATION: XYZ Paralegal Program, City, State.
December 1982.
Specialized in litigation and legal research.

New York University, New York, N.Y.
May, 1982. B.A. Double major in English and History.
                  Honors: Dean's List - 3 years.

EXPERIENCE:

September - December 1982   County Clerk's Office, Westchester County, N.Y. Court Aide. Assisted Deputy Chief County Clerk. Involved in all aspects of trial procedure.

Summer, 1982   Hilton Hotel, Tarrytown, N.Y. Storeroom Clerk. Responsible for inventory, requisitions, purchasing.

May - August 1981   Stephen's Van Lines, Irvington, N.Y. Shipping and receiving clerk. Maintained all shipping and receiving files. Responsible for inventory control and billing for major industrial warehouse.

1980 - 1981   Andrew's Floor Covering Company, Inc., Bronx, N.Y. Sales position in retail carpet and linoleum store. Job involved extensive personal and telephone contact with customers, salesmen, and wholesale distributers.

REFERENCES:
Furnished upon request.

Job Search

Once you have your résumé prepared, one-third of your job search is completed. You are now ready to begin to seek out the paralegal positions. Finding out about paralegal positions may take some perseverance, but the majority of graduates from reputable paralegal programs will find positions utilizing their training. The first point to bear in mind, is that 80 percent of jobs are *not* advertised. This means that these available positions are known only to those already working in the legal community. They are not positions advertised in the papers. This is important to remember since a paralegal graduate can become dismayed when looking in the classified advertisements every day and seeing only a few paralegal jobs listed. This does not mean that there are no jobs for paralegals. It just means that the paralegal positions are going to be filled either through contacts that the law firm or corporation has with paralegal programs, or through the résumés that are on file in the personnel offices. Thus it is imperative that you send your résumé to law firms and corporations even if they are not advertising for paralegals. Many lawyers keep résumés on file and will pull them out, instead of advertising in the newspaper, when a position becomes available in the office.

Another source of jobs will be the placement office of the paralegal programs. A paralegal program operating a good placement office will have an active and established relationship with the legal community. Lawyers like to go to paralegal programs for their graduates since paralegal programs, unlike employment agencies, do not charge the employer a fee. The placement office of a paralegal program will also screen its graduates for the type of background that the lawyer is requesting.

An active approach in looking for a paralegal job is best. Not only is it better for the student's self-esteem to be actively job searching on his/her own, but results will come faster if the student is sending out résumés to a carefully selected group of law firms and corporations.

The first step in looking for a paralegal job is to narrow down the number of places where your résumé can be sent. There are many places that a paralegal can send his/her résumé, but it is important to decide first on your geographical boundaries. If you

live in a large metropolitan area, how far do you want to com-
mute? How big a law firm or corporation do you want to work
for? And finally, before you go any further, give those places a call
to find out if they hire paralegals, and if so, to whom you should
address your résumé. The trick here is to get the name of the
person in charge of hiring so that you can address your letter
and envelope to him/her personally. You have a far better chance
of getting a response if you address your letter to a particular
person.

Getting the names and addresses of law firms is not at all
difficult. There is the lawyer's directory, *Martindale–Hubbell*,
which lists many firms and their lawyers. Included in the listings
are the telephone numbers of the firms, the names of many of
the partners and associates, plus the kind of law practiced
in the firm. If you have an interest in a particular kind of law
you might address a letter to the partner or department head
whose specialty it is. *Martindale–Hubbell* has several large
volumes, is up-dated yearly, and lists the firms alphabetically
according to state and city.

Corporate directories such as *Dun and Bradstreet* and *Standard and Poor*'s will give you the names and addresses of large
companies in the geographical area you are interested in working
in. A phone call to the general counsel or the personnel office
should furnish you with information on whether the company
hires paralegals, and to whom you should address a résumé.

Similarly, banks, insurance companies, and pension-consulting
firms will be listed either in trade magazines or the Yellow Pages
of the phone book. This research is most important in your letter-
writing campaign, since you will be doing this before mailing
out your résumés.

Every state has a law journal which is published daily. Once
or twice a year there will be a survey of law firms and corporations with salary information for lawyers, the number of
lawyers employed, and the number of paralegals employed. This
list can be extremely helpful in your job search as it will provide
you with the names of law firms and corporations that actually
hire paralegals. When you phone those places you will ask for the
name of the person in charge of hiring paralegals.

Some paralegal graduates seeking a job head first to an
employment agency hoping that the agency will conduct the entire
job search on their behalf. Usually this technique reaps meager
results. Most agencies are more attracted to paralegals with
significant work experience in a particular legal field since their

clients are seeking experienced paralegals. However, some agencies have a division for placement of paralegals on a temporary basis. I suggest a temporary position when the paralegal wants to sample different kinds of paralegal jobs to find the work setting most suited to his/her background. Usually the temporary paralegal work offered is more routine and task-oriented since it is "filling-in" on a big project which has an end in sight and does not justify hiring permanent employees. The paralegal is paid on an hourly basis by the agency and does not get any benefits. Some paralegals do find that this temporary work can evolve into permanent employment. At the very least though, the paralegal will gain work experience and references. And temporary work usually allows the paralegal to leave at any time for job interviews that may come up.

In suburban or rural areas, a paralegal graduate may find that the law practices are smaller, more self-contained, and the attorneys may not be completely sold on the idea of using a paralegal. Supplying the lawyers with written information concerning the economics of using paralegals is one idea, but some graduates find that working out a part-time schedule to demonstrate how effective their presence can be in the office is a more useful way of approaching this problem. Several years ago one paralegal graduate started out by working on a volunteer, part-time basis and shortly afterward was commanding $100 a day as a paralegal working in the same position!

Sending out cover letters with résumés is a very effective way of seeking a paralegal position (see pages 86–97 for "Cover Letter Format" and Model Letters). However, the follow-through of calling to inquire if the résumé was received and asking to set up an appointment to meet with a personnel director or a legal administrator is a sure way to show your real interest in working as a paralegal. It is difficult to say "no" to someone in person, even if it is on the telephone.

Very often, however, you will receive an acknowledgment of your résumé from the lawyer or legal administrator to whom the letter was addressed. The rule of thumb is that for every ten résumés you send out, you will receive one letter back requesting you to come in for an interview. The problem is that there is no way to guarantee that if you send out 100 résumés and letters that the 10 "positive" letters will come at the beginning of your letter-writing campaign rather than at the end! But the more letters you send out the more chances you have of getting interviews for paralegal positions.

Inevitably your first interview will materialize. Then comes the final part of your job search—and it is the interview which will clinch you the job!

Cover Letter Format

Address
City, State, Zip
Date

Name of Person, (Esq.) [if a lawyer]
Title
Name of Organization
Address
City, State, Zip

Dear

      Paragraph 1 – Reason for Writing

      Paragraph 2 – Summary of Qualifications
                (stated to show what you can
                  offer the law firm or organization)

      Paragraph 3 – Request for Interview

      Paragraph 4 – Thank you (optional)

                Very truly yours,
                  Signature
                Name

Interviews

Less than 10 percent of interviewing success is based on your educational background. Interviewing success is more likely to be linked to the first impression you make on the interviewer, the interviewer's perspective on how you will fit into the firm, your body language, facial expressions, and how you answer the interviewer's questions.

In order to prepare yourself thoroughly for each job interview, there are some important preparations you can make in order to ensure success. Successful job interviewing does not necessarily mean that you will get the job offer. Successful interviewing means that you were able to regard the interview as a

Sample Cover Letter

215 Rose Lane
Red Bank, New Jersey 07610

June 30, 1982

Richard Martinson, Esq.
Martinson & Vogel, P.C.
501 Fifth Avenue
New York, New York 10036

Dear Mr. Martinson:

    I have recently completed a baccalaureate degree in Paralegal Studies at ABC College. I am enclosing a copy of my resume in the hope that my training and work experiences can be utilized by your law firm.

    My major in Paralegal Studies combined with my junior year internship at a brokerage house has provided me with the skills necessary to be a competent legal assistant in a law firm which specializes in securities work. In addition, my summer employment as a bank teller provided me with practical experience in dealing with people.

    I hope to give you a call at the end of the month when I am in New York. If you should find my qualifications of interest to your firm, I would like to set up an appointment to meet with you.

Sincerely yours,

Raymond Silks

Enclosure

Sample Cover Letter

244 E. 89th Street
New York, New York 10028

August 9, 1983

Box 8245
The New York Times
229 West 43rd Street
New York, New York   10036

Dear Sir:

I am responding to your recent advertisement for a litigation paralegal. Enclosed please find a copy of my resume for your review.

I believe that I have the qualifications that you are seeking in a paralegal. I recently completed a certificate program in Paralegal Studies, specializing in litigation. My course work provided me with the necessary legal theory and procedural training to work effectively in trial preparation work. My previous position as a personnel assistant has given me the opportunity to develop good interviewing skills.

If you feel that my background is of interest to your firm, please feel free to contact me at either my work number or at my home.

Thank you for your consideration.

Sincerely yours,

Jeffrey B. Howe

Enclosure

means of finding out about the firm or corporation and whether or not the particular job is the right one for you. If you find that the available job is just what you are looking for but you get no job offer, then use that job as an example to recall when you interview the next time. If you get a job offer, but you decide that the job is not right for you, then use that same criterion when evaluating other job offers. It is important to remember that an interview is a two-way process: the interviewer wants to find out about you, but you want to find out if the job is right for you.

The request for you to interview comes either in the form of a letter or a phone call. When finding out about the interview, make sure that you know the name of the interviewer, the exact address (including room number, suite, or floor, such as is the case of the larger firms or companies), and the time of the interview. Write all of this information down as it is given to you so you can avoid a phone call back to check on the information.

Once you have the appointment, get busy with finding out about the employer. If it is a law firm, go to the public library or paralegal school library to check it out in *Martindale–Hubbell*. Find out how big the firm is, the kind of law that is practiced, and, if you are interviewing with one of the attorneys in the firm, check his/her biographical data. From these listings you can find out birthdate, college, law school, publications, and areas of law that the attorney has specialized in. All of this information can be used by you in the interview to assure the interviewer that you are interested in him/her and in the firm itself.

If the interview is with a corporation, use a corporate directory to research the company. Public libraries and your paralegal program should have such directories. You will find the company's assets, products, subsidiaries, and divisions. You might also see if the company has a public relations department which publishes brochures about it. Annual reports are another source of valuable information about corporations. It is extremely important to know something about the law firm or company, because inevitably you will be asked what you know about the employer during the interview.

Once you know something about the firm or company, dress the part of an employee there. In other words, there is probably a different way of dressing in a law firm, corporation, bank, insurance company, and public sector job in your part of the country. A rule of thumb is that generally dress in the private sector is more formal than in the public sector. Part of the interviewing process, remember, is to see whether you fit into the structure of the office, so dressing the part of the job while on the interview will put you in good stead.

In the private sector's large law firms, banks, and insurance companies, conservative dress is the rule. It is recommended that a man be clean shaven, wear a dark suit (gray or navy blue), a white shirt, and a muted-toned tie. Shoes should be polished. A woman should wear a skirt-suit or a blazer and skirt, plain blouse, neutral-colored stockings, closed-toed shoes, and a simple hair-do. A minimal amount of jewelry and no perfume are the rule.

To complete these "uniforms," a briefcase is a necessity, it symbolizes that you are a professional. Lawyers carry briefcases and so should paralegals. You may not have much to carry in your briefcase at first, but you should have extra copies of your résumé, writing samples, and the names of your references with you for an interview. Women may find it handy to keep their purses in their briefcases or use their briefcases as purses in order to eliminate carrying around extra items.

Do not arrive more than ten minutes early for your interview. Walk around the block a few times to relax if you arrive at your destination with more than ten minutes to spare. The reason for this is that by arriving too early for your appointment and having to wait around in the reception area, you are bound to attract attention to yourself from either the receptionist or other employees of the firm or company. Of course if you are going to be a few minutes late, you call to let the interviewer know.

When you arrive at the reception area, or office, give your name, and reason for your appointment, and the name of the person with whom you are interviewing. You might also want to give the time of your appointment to make it easier for the receptionist. The receptionist will usually ask you to take a seat and will contact the interviewer for you. When the interviewer comes over to greet you, stand up and shake hands with him/her. The interviewer will lead you into an office where the interview will take place.

Most interviewers have a definite idea of how they want the interview to proceed, so allow the interviewer to take the lead. He/she will tell you which chair to sit in, for instance. There is usually more than one chair in an office, and on occasion the other chair will be used by another interviewer in a "group interview." Your briefcase goes on the floor next to you within easy reach. Never put anything on the interviewer's desk!

Interviews generally begin with "small talk." Questions posed to you in the beginning of an interview might range from "Did you have any trouble finding us?" to "How did you find out about the firm?" You would never answer questions such as these with replies of: "I had the worst time trying to find you" or, "Oh, I just looked up the firm in *Martindale–Hubbell* and you were part of my mass mailing to law firms." Answers like the above would indicate to the interviewer that you have very little regard for the interview since you spent little or no time researching the firm before you applied to it. Better answers would be: "I know the location of your firm very well. I have been in this area several times," and, "I applied to your firm because I have a particular interest in real estate law and I understand that your firm has expertise in this field."

Generally the next part of the interview will consist of a routine rundown of items on your résumé. Needless to say, you must know your résumé inside and out. Sometimes people forget how they worded certain parts of their résumés. So be prepared to comment on a point and add to it if the interviewer asks you something about a prior job.

The next part of the interview will usually consist of your answering direct questions about why you studied to become a paralegal, what your future career goals are, and what kind of job you are looking for. Included here is a list of some of the questions that paralegal clients have been asked during interviews.

Questions Frequently Asked During an Interview

(Familiarize yourself with answers to these questions)

- What are your qualifications as a paralegal?
- Why did you specialize in the area of real estate? (or other legal area)
- What does a paralegal do?
- How are your research skills?
- Do you have any children?
- What kind of salary are you seeking?
- What did you study in your paralegal program?
- Why are you better than your competition?
- Why are you making a career change?
- What is your marital status?

Knowing how to answer questions asked by the interviewer is the key to interviewing success.

- Can you give the law firm a two-year commitment?
- What didn't you like about your last position?
- Are you planning on going to law school?
- Can you type?
- Can you work over-time?
- Tell me about yourself.

Answer all questions to the point. Keep your answers succinct and clear. Sometimes when nervous you might have the habit of rambling on a bit, but a job interview is no place for this.

The interviewer will usually ask you if you have any questions about the firm. Remember again that this job interview is the opportunity for you to learn about the firm or the company and find out if the job is right for you, so have a few questions ready to ask the interviewer. Questions you might ask could include: how many paralegals are employed; what is the general length of time that paralegals stay at the firm; are there opportunities to learn other areas of law at the firm or company?

Do not bring up salary as one of *your* questions. If you do, it appears as though that is the *only* reason you are looking for a paralegal position. It is the interviewer who will usually bring up the subject of salary. He/she might state what the firm is offering or ask you what kind of salary you are looking for. If he/she asks you the salary you want, always give a salary *range*. Never give a set dollar amount since it might be more than what they are offering and disqualify you immediately, or it might be far less than what they are offering and you would be settling for less. The going rate for paralegals with formal training and no work experience in 1982 is between $13,000 and $15,000 per year. This does not include bonuses. Depending on the law firm or company, the part of the country you live in, and, of course, other qualifications you have (such as speaking another language fluently or having prior legal experience) this salary would be negotiable.

If the interviewer tells you during the interview what the job's salary is, and asks you what you think of it, do not debate the amount. Simply say that you will consider the salary but since there is no job offer there is no point in discussing the amount. Many people make the mistake of discussing the salary for a job that has not been offered to them. Do not discuss the salary until you get a firm offer and the job is yours. If the salary is less than what you expected, then tell the interviewer that you are worth more because of your prior education or experience. Do not say that you could not possibly live on the amount they offered you. Unfortunately employers do not care what kind of salary you can live on. But they cannot argue that you are not worth the amount that you say you are, as long as it is a reasonable amount. What happens in some cases is that the firm will negotiate with you for a salary review after three months or so.

What about settling for less money than what you expected? If you can afford it, in your first job as a paralegal it may not be too bad since you will be getting that golden experience you need to succeed in the field. (Do not forget that as soon as you get your first paralegal job, your résumé immediately has to be updated to include your new experience.) Also, the firm may offer paid overtime so you could increase your salary by working overtime as needed. And, of course, you may make yourself so indispensable to the firm that you may warrant a big raise in the future.

Some firms and companies pay a higher salary but expect you to work overtime when needed. In this respect they are treating you as they do the attorneys. This is a good sign that the firm has no doubt that you are a professional.

Civil rights legislation makes it illegal for a prospective employer to ask certain questions about age, marital status, race, place of national origin, etc. Some interviewers will ask you personal questions that might be illegal. You do *not* have to answer those questions and you might even want to tell the interviewer this, but by doing so you might be talking yourself out of a job. If a question comes up regarding marital status or children, answer the questions in a positive fashion by stating that you are able to commit yourself to a career. "I am married and able to commit myself to a career. I am divorced and am able to commit myself to a career. I have three children and am able to commit myself to a career." Usually when the interviewer asks those kinds of questions he/she is trying to discover if there are any obstacles to your coming into the office every day before hiring you. But if the questions begin to make you feel uncomfortable then perhaps you should evaluate the job situation and consider whether you really want to work in this firm, or with the individual who is asking you these personal questions. Again, this is another example of finding out if the job is right for you.

You may be asked where else you have interviewed. It is always a good idea to say that you are waiting to hear from a few places that you applied to (you do not have to give out the names). If this is your first interview, say that you have just begun to look. Firms and companies want to know what their competition is and you should let them know, when possible, that other places are also seeking you out.

Sometimes other attorneys or paralegals will be asked to join in on the interview. This is called a "Group Interview" and can be disconcerting the first time. Some firms feel that by having more than one person interview the applicant the decision to hire can be made faster because there is more input. Having those extra copies of your résumé will come in handy. Do make sure that you offer those résumés to the people who join the interview. Try to remember the names of the people as they are introduced to you. Jotting down their names on a pad is not a bad idea since you will probably be sending them thank-you notes after the interview. Maintain eye contact throughout the interview. It is very important.

Some firms consider a tour around the offices as a part of the interview. This gives you the opportunity to see the set-up for paralegals. Note whether paralegals share offices or have their own offices. This is all part of the work environment that you will want to consider.

At the end of the interview, many students will offer the interviewer a copy of a writing sample with a self-addressed, stamped envelope so that it can be mailed back. This is an excellent idea since it is an example of your work. Most attorneys are glad to have the opportunity to look over the sample.

The interviewer will let you know when the interview is over. Shake hands with him/her, tell him/her how you enjoyed meeting with him/her, thank him/her for his/her time, and ask when you might be hearing about the decision. Show interest, although you may have decided at the midpoint of the interview that the job is not for you. This is important because even if you are disappointed in the job but are offered it, there may be another opening in the firm that you could be considered for at a later date.

When you get home, write out all your impressions of the interview. Keep this for future reference when you are comparing interviews with firms and companies. Then write or type a thank-you note to each person who interviewed you, telling each that you enjoyed the meeting. If you think the job is right for you and you would be an asset to the firm, write that. A sample thank-you note on page 97 is included as a model to follow.

Continue to send out résumés while you are waiting to hear about the job. Usually you will get an answer within the time you were told it would take. If you do not, wait an extra day, and then contact the firm or company to find out what your status is. There is nothing wrong with this and it tells them that you are really interested in the job.

When that job offer comes in, consider the job for a few days. Remember, this is a big commitment to both the firm and yourself and should be a job in which you will be able to grow and learn. When you are ready to accept the job, a phone call to them will suffice but follow up with a letter stating that you are accepting the job. Include the stated salary in the letter. Ask them for a letter noting your starting date and the salary agreed upon. This is for your protection as well as theirs. On occasion, the person who hired you and told you what your salary would be is no longer working for the firm or company when you begin the job. Having something in writing is a very good idea.

Most firms and companies will expect you to begin to work for them within two weeks after you receive and accept the job offer. If you are working at another job and need to give notice, and the notice will be more than two weeks, clear this up with your new place of employment. By following the rules of your old company you will be giving your new employer a good impression of you.

Once you secure that first job as a paralegal, your career has begun!

Model Follow-Up Thank You Note to Interviewer

69 Park Road
Red Bank, New Jersey 07102

June 23, 1983

Roberta Mitchell, Esq.
Mitchell & Schwartzman, P.C.
936 Forest Avenue
Buffalo, New York   14222

Dear Ms. Mitchell:

Thank you for meeting with me on Friday. I enjoyed our discussion about your law firm and the position of a real estate paralegal. The job seems very interesting to me and I believe that I have the background and skills you are seeking in a legal assistant.

I look forward to hearing from you.

Sincerely yours,

Lawrence S. Lane

6. Your First Day on the Job

Many recently graduated paralegals start their first day on the job uncertain of what to expect. These uncertainties concern how they will be viewed by the other staff and/or utilized as a member of the legal team. It is important to remember that starting a paralegal job is like starting any other new job for which you received educational training; your first several weeks are a "getting acquainted" period with the staff. Paralegal training does differ from program to program and many lawyers are still experimenting with how to use paralegals most effectively.

Prepare in Advance

Before your first day of work, review your notes and textbook readings from your paralegal training program to familiarize yourself with the legal terminology and procedures that you were taught, since there may have been some time between your graduation and your first day on the job. It is best to refresh your memory by reading over these course materials.

You may find that your first position involves work in an area of law with which you are not familiar. If so, ask one of your former instructors to recommend a book or two in that area of law so that you can do some homework, which will make you feel more confident on your first day.

In addition to preparing for the type of law which is practiced by your new employer, it is also a good idea to do some in-depth research about your new place of employment if you did not do so before your interview. If it is a law firm, then go back to their listing in *Martindale–Hubbell*. Become familiar with the names, backgrounds, and areas of legal expertise of the firm's lawyers. This will assist you in feeling more at ease with the lawyers you meet on the first day.

If your first job is in the legal department of a corporation, you should go to *Standard and Poor's* or *Dun and Bradstreet* and acquaint yourself with the company's size, products, divisions, subsidiaries, and locations. Such information can help give you confidence, make you more useful in the first week or two of the job, and demonstrate to your new bosses that you *are* interested in your new job.

Government agencies frequently have annual reports and pamphlets prepared to inform the public of their functions. Pay a visit to the agency to pick up some of this information before you begin your employment. The facts that you learn by reading through the reports and pamphlets will demonstrate to the other staff that you are interested and concerned about your new position.

You may want to pay a visit to your new place of employment before you start on the job. You can meet informally with the lawyers and paralegals before starting work. You can introduce yourself to your fellow employees and ask any questions about the work setting, and types of law that you will become involved in. Sometimes this is done before accepting the job offer, however, it's easy to forget about it in the excitement of accepting the job offer. Taking the opportunity to make a short informal visit before beginning the job is perfectly acceptable and is usually recommended.

Dress for the first day on the job as you dressed for the interview (see page 90 for suggestions). It is always possible that once you begin the job you will find that the legal staff dresses casually and you may wish to follow suit. But on the first day of the job you should always dress somewhat more formally; it can only make a better first impression with the lawyers.

Allow extra time for getting ready on the morning of the first day of the job since you will probably want to arrive a half-hour earlier than usual. First, you want to be certain that you know how to get to the job (don't be late!). Second, you will need some extra time in the morning to meet with the person in charge of personnel.

If you received a letter confirming your position at an agreed upon salary, you should bring it with you on the first day. You should also bring with you several more copies of your résumé. Many personnel offices need a résumé on file for each employee. The résumé that was sent in for your interview may have been written on and/or kept by one of the attorneys who interviewed you.

You will probably be asked to fill out numerous forms on your first day. These forms may include an application for employment, as well as health and insurance forms. Some companies may also expect you to have a physical examination by the company doctor. The numbers that you will need to have on hand may include your Social Security number, your spouse's Social Security number, telephone number of your spouse's place of employment, telephone numbers of your references, and the numbers and names of your health insurance policies. You may also be given a booklet on the office's policies in regard to vacations, sick days, personal days, and overtime.

Next, the personnel director or the attorney with whom you will be working most closely will escort you around the offices to introduce you to the other staff members. You will also be shown the typing and stenography pools, the word-processing area, the law library, the file room, and the firm's or company's dining room, if there is one. You will also be instructed on how to fill out your daily time records.

Either before or after your tour of the office you will be shown to your own office.

Many paralegals start in their jobs by sharing an office with other paralegals. In fact, many attorneys will also share an office if the law firm has a problem with office space. The advantages of sharing an office are that you will not feel isolated during your training period. You will usually have someone close by to answer your questions. You will also have the opportunity to develop some camaraderie with the other paralegal staff.

The disadvantage of sharing an office is that you may have distractions or noise when you are trying to complete an assignment which requires deep concentration. Or you may have some problems when making phone calls to clients or interviewing clients in person.

The law library or the conference room, when not in use, may be the place where you might want to relocate temporarily when there are too many distractions in your office. Remember, as you become a more senior member of the paralegal staff there is always the possibility of being moved to an office of your own if the space is available.

Your space within the office, whether or not you are sharing it with other paralegals, will have a desk, chair, and phone. Usually there will also be a bookcase nearby for you to store some of your paralegal texts. The bookcase can also be used to store some of

the case files you may be using when you assist an attorney on a case.

Some paralegals share a secretary with another attorney or with another paralegal. Usually the secretary will be next to your office in order to facilitate your bringing work for him/her to type. In other law offices, paralegals may use only the typing pool to assist them in their work.

Many lawyers will take their new paralegals out to lunch on their first day as a "welcome to the office" gesture. In some offices the existing paralegal staff may take the new paralegal out.

Ask Questions

One of the most common concerns of a novice paralegal is what he/she will be expected to do during his/her first few months on the job. Will he/she be given a complex assignment with few or no instructions and be expected to handle it on his/her own? How much of the paralegal's training will be applicable to the job?

Most attorneys will not give difficult or complicated assignments to a new paralegal. There can be an exception, of course, as in the case of the paralegal described in Chapter 7, who was given a pension plan to work on during her first week of employment. If you are given an assignment which you do not understand or are unsure of, ask to be shown how to complete it. It is extremely important that you ask a lot of questions during your training period. It is part of the training process and the lawyers expect it. Remember, too, that all of your work will always be reviewed by an attorney.

The key to becoming a competent paralegal is to ask questions, to be unafraid of making a mistake, and to learn through your errors. By feeling prepared to start work as a paralegal, and knowing what you can expect on the job, you should be able to begin your paralegal career on the right footing.

7. Other Career Opportunities Utilizing Paralegal Training and Experience

There are many paralegals working in the public, private, or nonprofit sectors, who intend to stay in their positions and will be looking forward to job security and financial rewards. However, some people who graduate from paralegal programs eventually decide to use their training in careers other than the legal profession.

In Education

Educators frequently take paralegal courses and apply the law and legal concepts in their social studies, American history, or sociology classes. Their legal training will supplement and enhance their subject area knowledge and teaching experience. He/she can bring into the classroom such learning strategies as voir dire, moot courts, and writing briefs. Attorneys, judges, and police can talk to the classes to help students understand how lawyers and law enforcement people participate in the criminal justice system. Such classes are part of the curriculum in many school districts.

People with paralegal training may find employment as administrators or teachers in a paralegal studies program. Experienced paralegals may find positions as program directors, placement directors, and instructors. The number of available positions may be limited since there are approximately 300 paralegal programs in existence.

A program director who trained and worked as a paralegal is very familiar with the profession and can provide assistance to a new and developing program. A director is responsible for the advertising of the program, the recruitment and interviewing of the students, and overseeing the other administrative details in program management.

A placement director is responsible for employment orientations, job development, and may act as a liaison between the employer and the paralegal graduate seeking a position.

A paralegal instructor is responsible for teaching paralegal students the legal procedures used by paralegals in law offices.

Corporate Legal Services

Paralegals are also employed in companies that provide corporate legal services to law firms and corporations. These companies serve the legal profession throughout the United States and in some foreign countries. Paralegals have daily contact with the companies' clients, the lawyers.

There are few such companies in existence. One is the Prentice-Hall Corporation System, Inc., located in all fifty states, Puerto Rico, Liberia, and Panama. Its executive offices are in New York City.

The Prentice-Hall Corporation System furnishes services enabling lawyers to organize, maintain, dissolve, consolidate, or merge corporations. It furnishes the statutory agent for domestic or foreign corporations in any state.

These processes involve on-going relationships among law firms, corporations, and the Prentice-Hall Corporation System. Paralegals assist in providing complete and up-to-date corporate information to the clients.

A paralegal seeking a position with a company that provides corporate legal services will find that they offer a congenial atmosphere not always found in large law firms, and his/her training and experience in corporations and securities will be fully utilized.

Salaries vary for entry-level paralegals. Currently the figure is close to what is being paid in medium-sized law firms.

Legal Publishing Houses

Legal publishing companies are another source of employment for paralegals. They use paralegals to assist the general counsel in the company's legal department with the areas of law that affect publishing, such as contract law and copyright law. There are also positions in other parts of the company for persons who possess paralegal training or experience and who also have strong writing and oral communication skills.

Paralegals may work as consultants or advisors to legal publishing houses. They may assist the legal publisher in planning new kinds of books to be written either about the paralegal profession or the procedures utilized by paralegals in law offices. Paralegals may also serve as recruiters of authors for new materials to be published.

Paralegals with college degrees in English may also be used as proofreaders and editors. Their background and knowledge of legal terminology would prove helpful when reviewing the content of law-related manuscripts.

Persons with paralegal training and sales experience can work in the marketing division of legal publishing companies. An exposure to law and legal thinking as well as sales experience can enable marketing representatives to earn high commissions when selling law-related books.

8. Should You Eventually Go to Law School?

Attending law school is a three- or four-year commitment after completion of your bachelor's degree. If you choose to attend law school on a full-time basis during the day, it will take you three years to complete. If you choose to attend on a part-time basis (as many people with full-time jobs do), you will complete law school in four years by going to classes in the evenings.

The other major factor is the expense. Tuition alone in many of the nation's law schools is over $6,000 a year. This does not include room, board, living expenses, and books. With the cuts in aid for graduate students, this can prove to be a financial hardship for those who wish to attend law school. There are some scholarships available for students with exceptional grades, for members of minority groups, and for students with severe economic need and high undergraduate cumulative averages.

Taking the Law School Admission Test

Entrance to law schools is highly competitive. Although there is no particular major which is required, your undergraduate academic record must be good. You also must achieve a certain score on the Law School Admission Test (LSAT), which will vary from law school to law school. The test is graded on a scale from ten to fifty. The LSAT will test your abilities in logical reasoning, analytical reasoning, reading comprehension, rules, and questions. In addition, you will be asked to furnish a writing sample during the test.

The examination is given four times a year: February, June, October, and December. The application for the LSAT can be picked up from any college or university, career counseling or placement office, or you may write directly to:

Law School Admission Services
Box 2000
Newtown, PA 18940
215-968-1100

Some students feel that their scores can be improved by taking an LSAT preparation course. These courses are offered through colleges and universities for a fee and by proprietary test preparation centers. The courses focus on improving the requisite skills needed for the examination: logic, analytical reasoning, reading comprehension, and writing ability. There may also be an emphasis on timing techniques since the LSAT is a timed examination.

The courses vary in price, from $135 for an eighteen-hour weekend course to $375 for an eight-week session. Most of the test preparation centers will provide you with course materials and counseling services. Many of them also tape record their lectures so you can listen to them again at your convenience. Some of the centers have a guarantee that you may take the preparatory course again for free if you are dissatisfied with your test score. Some law school applicants find it useful to study test preparation books containing sample examinations.

Applying to Law Schools

There are several guides to law schools available. These books can be purchased from bookstores or borrowed from libraries. Many college placement offices also have copies of these books. The information found in these guides includes the school's address, a description of the facilities, the law library, the faculty, and indicates the average LSAT score and cumulative grade point average held by their freshman class. This information will give you an idea of the schools to which you can apply with a reasonable chance of being accepted. (You should allow yourself ample time to pursue the information before making decisions about where to apply.)

You should begin preparing to apply to law school approximately a year before you actually do so. It is important to send away for the school's catalogs and applications well ahead of the time that material is actually due at the school's admissions office.

Application procedures will include completing the appropriate forms from the law schools, submitting references, and writing an essay. You may be able to request an interview with the admissions officers at some law schools.

You should apply to at least ten law schools. Some of these should be "safe" schools and some should be schools where you may have a borderline chance of being accepted.

Law School Curricula

Most law schools have a prescribed course of study for their first-year students. The courses will include: contract law, real property, civil procedure, criminal law, constitutional law, business corporations, and legal research and writing. In the second and third years the students will choose electives to complement their other requirements.

Law school itself can prove to be a competitive and pressure-oriented experience since the emphasis is on extensive assigned readings, preparation of briefs on cases, independent study, and lengthy writing assignments. In addition there are moot court and writing competitions. Students who do exceptionally well within courses are often selected to do additional work on a law review (a general legal publication). Writing competitions are also a means to achieve a place on the schools' journals, which are edited and published by its members. In addition to the law review, journals can concentrate on specific areas of law such as international law, urban law, and immigration law.

Students also seek law-related employment during the summers between law school terms. Their summer jobs, law school grades, and their outside activities, such as being an editor of a law review or a law journal, or working as an unpaid intern in a legal clinic, can be instrumental in the success that a law school graduate will have in securing permanent employment as a lawyer after he/she graduates from law school.

People who desire to become attorneys usually are interested in the judicial system, intelligent, hard-working, and capable of analyzing complex facts. People who are interested in working as paralegals have the same characteristics. Undoubtedly many of the people who train to become paralegals will consider law school as another career alternative after working in a legal setting.

Many lawyers were formerly paralegals, either graduates from formal training programs or trained in-house by law firms. This crossover is common.

Some former paralegals decide to go on to law school.

Profile—Paralegal Who Became a Lawyer

Pat M. studied at a college in Ohio to become an elementary school teacher. Upon graduation in 1970 she secured a teaching position and all signs pointed to her having a career in education.

Within a year everything changed. As a young teacher Pat was one of the first to experience the budget cuts which affected the teaching profession. The cutbacks and layoffs resulting from the loss of government funding, and the closing of schools, left her unemployed.

Pat had never considered a career in law until a friend suggested that she seek retraining as a paralegal. The paralegal training program she chose offered a seventeen-week general practice course. This seemed attractive to her since she would be prepared for a new career in a short period of time.

After completing the program she interviewed with a sole practitioner who was eager to use a paralegal in his office along with his part-time secretary.

The first assignment that Pat received from her employer was to put together a pension plan for one of the firm's clients. This doctor's pension plan had been laying untouched on the attorney's desk for over eighteen months before Pat began to work at the firm.

The attorney, never having used a paralegal before, assumed that Pat could work on the pension plan with little or no assistance from him. He did furnish her with a sample plan to use as an example.

It took Pat three weeks working alone to complete the plan. When the plan was accepted by the Internal Revenue Service shortly after it was submitted, her employer asked her if she would like to become an attorney. He said that he was willing to sponsor her as a law clerk in his office.

Pat was pleased since under this plan she would not have to attend law school. Instead she would clerk for five years and if she passed the state bar examination she would become an attorney.

It is important to know that only very few states accept law clerk training as a substitute for attendance at law school. In September 1973 the law changed in New York State, the state where Pat was working as a law clerk. But Pat was fortunate to be covered by the grandfather clause in that law, permitting law clerks already being trained as attorneys to continue the process. In January 1973, the Court of Appeals of the State of New York sent Pat and her employer a Certificate of Commencement of Office Study.

The only information that Pat had to provide to the Court of Appeals was her name, address, age, whether she had ever been a law secretary, and for how long, and whether she was a college graduate. Her employer also had to attest that Pat had never taken more than a month's vacation in any of the years that she clerked.

During those five years of working as a law clerk, Pat performed extensive paralegal duties, utilizing her formal paralegal education.

She took a bar review course after clerking for two years to become familiar with the kinds of questions that would be present in the bar examination.

After her years of clerking were over, Pat took another bar review course and passed the bar examination on the first try. She was approved by the Character Committee and was sworn in as an attorney along with other young lawyers who had graduated from law school. She is now practicing law as a partner with her sponsor.

Only a few states allow a person to become an attorney by clerking. New York State, for instance, now requires that a law clerk successfully complete one year of law school and clerk for four years under a sponsoring attorney who must provide the clerk with structured paralegal courses.

To obtain information about clerking in lieu of law school or by completing only one year of law school, contact the court in your state which is responsible for admitting attorneys to practice. There are also state statutes which regulate the admission of attorneys to practice.

Pat did not attend law school to become an attorney. Some paralegals do eventually decide to go to law school to become attorneys. If you are undecided about a law career but would like to study some law or work in a legal setting to find out what it is like, taking a paralegal training program could be step one in determining your career. Although the training received in paralegal programs is not as rigorous as that given in law schools, the concepts, theories, written assignments, legal research, and reading materials are similar. There are also internships available to paralegal students enabling them to work on a volunteer basis in the public interest sector, and sometimes also in private law offices.

Some students who excel in paralegal programs decide to apply directly to law schools without ever seeking employment as a paralegal. The education they received in paralegal courses will be helpful to them in law school, especially the legal research and writing courses. Since the application procedures for law schools include references, students may find that their instructors can provide recommendations for them and also be able to comment on their ability to learn about and understand the law. Taking a paralegal course, however, is not considered to be a "steppingstone" into law school.

Other paralegals work in law offices to help them decide whether they wish to make the commitment to attend law school. A paralegal who is exposed to a variety of legal problems will have a better idea of what working as a lawyer will entail. He/she will also have opportunities to talk to lawyers in the office about the practice of law.

Some corporations have tuition reimbursement plans. Paralegals working in a corporation may find that their law school education can be paid for by the company. These paralegals may wish to attend law school in the evenings after work for a total of four years.

When a paralegal has worked in a law office and decides to go to law school, he/she will usually find that the lawyers he/she works with have mixed feelings. The dilemma for the law office is that it is losing a competent and highly skilled legal assistant who must be replaced. But the lawyers will also realize that this is a major step in the paralegal's career and is of great importance to him/her.

Some law firms will accept their former paralegals as summer employees between law school semesters. Others will allow the paralegals to continue to work on a part-time basis while attending law school. Some may offer the former paralegal a position as an associate when he/she completes law school. Of course there is never any guarantee that the law firm will offer you anything but their good wishes for your success as a lawyer.

Whatever happens, having worked as a paralegal can only assist you in finding employment as a lawyer. The skills and knowledge you attained by performing paralegal duties will help to make you a well-qualified lawyer.

An adult of any age can study to become an attorney. There is no age cut-off for entering law school. For this reason becoming a lawyer can be as attractive to a person making a career change as to one starting out.

Always keep in mind that paralegals are lawyer's assistants. They must always work under the supervision of a lawyer and have limitations on the kinds of duties they can perform. They cannot give legal advice nor can they act as advocates for the law firm's clients. They also cannot share in the law firm's profits.

Paralegalism, however, is a career which offers prestige, professional status, and financial security. It definitely is a profession that gives its members many of the same intrinsic satisfactions that an attorney experiences.

9. The Future for Paralegals

As the legal profession moves into the twenty-first century there will be increasingly more complex legal issues confronting our society. The paralegal's role in assisting the attorney will expand as the practice of law includes the increased use of computer technology.

Advanced Technology

The legal profession's use of computers and other technological equipment has grown over the last several years. Paralegals are emerging as some of the trained operators of the computer terminals.

Complex litigation is one area of law which has seen an increased use of computers as a means of controlling the documents. Litigation paralegals working on a large antitrust case, for example, must handle thousands and thousands of documents. Computer storage systems can make the storage and retrieval of documents much more manageable than by conventional methods.

The paralegals would be responsible for analyzing and coding the documents and depositions, and searching for and retrieving the data from the computer memory. Usually there are project managers trained to ensure quality control who supervise teams of paralegals engaged in such projects.

In addition there are consulting groups which assist attorneys in choosing computer software and hardware, analyzing the vendors and data techniques, and designing the systems needed to produce the information. A litigation support system includes time-shared computer data bases which can be reached through a telecommunications network.

Law library management is another area where computer technology has established a foothold. Law firms are beginning to automate their specialty area internal memoranda of law. Another area presently undergoing development is the "boilerplate" library where standard forms used in estate, real estate, and contract matters are put into information banks. Paralegals are needed to become managers of these libraries.

Computerized legal research is another area where a paralegal may play an essential role. Westlaw™ and LEXIS™ are two of the most commonly used data bases. These data bases are used in law firms, corporations, banks, insurance companies, and even in law schools. Both of these systems have been developed to enable the legal profession to perform legal research thoroughly and quickly. The traditional method of conducting legal research very often involves many attorney or paralegal hours spent in a law library. With computerized legal research systems, such work can be performed in a shorter period of time, thereby saving money for the client.

A paralegal who is experienced and competent in performing legal research can effectively operate a computer-assisted legal research system. He/she may be called a research assistant or an information specialist.

A paralegal trained to operate a terminal can cite-check, shepardize, and retrieve information. Training courses are available for personnel of law firms and other corporations that utilize computerized legal research systems.

The companies that design and install legal research computers also employ paralegals. With their understanding of legal terminology and legal research, paralegals can serve as marketing analysts, sales representatives, and system programmers.

Supervisory Positions

As law practices expand their use of paralegals, paralegals are assuming the supervisory roles as law office administrators and senior legal assistants.

Law Office Administration

The American Bar Association's Special Committee on Legal

Assistants set forth a variety of tasks that can be performed by law office administrators and managers. The tasks include designing, developing and planning new procedures, techniques, services, processes, and applications in the office; planning, supervising, and assisting in the installation and maintenance of relatively complex office equipment; and planning productions, operations of services for the efficient use of manpower materials, money, and equipment in the office.

Managing a firm can be time-consuming and expensive for lawyers to handle on their own, so law office management and administration is a career opportunity for experienced nonlawyer personnel. Many of the large corporate law firms in the country are now utilizing persons with management and legal experience as administrators. Many of the smaller law firms are using office managers to assist the managing partners.

Some paralegal training programs offer courses in law office management. Students would become familiar with management concepts, types of law practices, and various systems used in the office. Students would learn about time keeping and billing procedures; legal fees; personnel administration of the nonlawyer staff; special administration systems, such as filing, billing, and purchasing, computer technology, and word-processing equipment; and effective use of legal secretaries, case aides, and paralegals.

At the present time, a law office administrator can be referred to by several different titles: office administrator, business manager, office manager, or legal administrator.

A law office administrator reports directly to the managing partners of the law firm. He/she also meets with administration committees in the law firm. In his/her reports with these lawyers he/she would be required to provide specific financial and management information. He/she may also prepare budgets and allocate monies for equipment and supplies.

The law office administrator has the responsibility and the authority in personnel matters involving the nonlawyer staff. This may include interviewing, hiring, and firing; training; writing performance evaluations; assigning work; allocating equipment; and disciplining employees.

In some firms he/she may be in charge of devising filing systems and developing a training manual for the nonlawyer staff.

Law office administrators earn from the high teens to over $50,000 a year.

A paralegal job can be a rewarding and challenging career.

Senior Legal Assistants

The need for senior legal assistants has grown along with the paralegal profession in order to develop policies concerning control, delegation of work, coordination of work flow, and career advancement for paralegals.

Becoming a senior legal assistant is a major career step for a paralegal. Promotion to senior legal assistant is usually done from within a paralegal staff, based on the criteria that the paralegal must have excellent performance reviews while working at least three years at the firm and be a college graduate. Salaries will range from $25,000 to $45,000 a year.

These professionals are responsible for overseeing the work of other paralegals in the firm. This is usually done on a departmental basis. For example, a senior legal assistant in the real estate department would only supervise the work of the other paralegals in his/her department.

Specific job duties for senior legal assistants include delegating work, ensuring that the work is distributed equally and fairly, handling personnel related problems in the department, writing appraisals of the other paralegals, and supervising the hiring of paralegals when needed. This would also include directing the specialized training needed when a new paralegal joins the staff.

Senior legal assistants may work as paralegals only 50 percent of the time. Their managerial responsibilities and work on special projects, such as setting up billing systems, would take up the remainder of their time at the office.

Appendix 1. Paralegal Training Programs

The programs marked with an asterisk indicate American Bar Association final approval. Although every attempt was made to provide an up-to-date list of paralegal programs and those with American Bar Association approval, there may be some new programs which developed and some other programs which attained American Bar Association approval after this book was published.

The guidelines established by the American Bar Association to grant approval to paralegal programs are evaluative in nature. Seeking American Bar Association approval is a voluntary effort initiated by the paralegal program. It involves an on-site visitation by representatives from the Standing Committee on Legal Assistants as well as the program's submission of a detailed self-evaluation report.

This list was compiled by the American Bar Association.

Alabama

Auburn University
Legal Assistant Education
Department of Justice and
    Public Safety
Montgomery, AL 36193

*Samford University
Division of Paralegal Studies
Birmingham, AL 35209

Southern Institute
2015 Highland Avenue
Birmingham, AL 35205

Spring Hill College
Legal Studies Program
Mobile, AL 36608

University of South Alabama
Division of C.E. and Evening
    Studies
307 University Boulevard
Mobile, AL 36688

Alaska

Juneau–Douglas Community
    College
Division of Business–Paralegal
    Studies Program
P.O. Box 1447
Juneau, AK 99802

University of Alaska–Anchorage
Anchorage Community College
Law Science Program
2533 Providence Avenue
Anchorage, AK 99501

Arizona

Arizona State University
Paralegal Program
Department of Administrative
    Services
Tempe, AZ 85281

*Northern Arizona University
Legal Assistant Program
Box 15044
Flagstaff, AZ 86011

Paralegal Institute
1315 West Indian
School Drawer 33903
Phoenix, AZ 85067

Phoenix College
Department of Business
1202 West Thomas Road
Phoenix, AZ 85013

Scottsdale Community College
9000 East Chapparral
Scottsdale, AZ 85253

Sterling School
1010 East Indian School Road
Phoenix, AZ 85014

California

American College of Paramedical
  Arts and Sciences
1800 North Broadway
Santa Ana, CA 92706

American Legal Services
  Institute
c/o 2719 Canada Boulevard
Glendale, CA 91208

American River College
4700 College Oak Drive
Sacramento, CA 95841

California College of Paralegal
  Studies
6832 Van Nuys Boulevard
Van Nuys, CA 91405

California State College,
  San Bernardino
Paralegal Studies
Department of Political Science
550 State College Parkway
San Bernardino, CA 92407

California State University,
  Chico
Chico, CA 95929

California State University,
  Dominguez Hills
Public Paralegal Certificate
  Program
School of Social and Behavioral
  Sciences
Carson, CA 90747

*California State University at
  Los Angeles
Certification Program for the
  Legal Assistant
5151 State University Drive
Los Angeles, CA 90032

Canada College
4200 Farm Hill Boulevard
Redwood City, CA 94061

Cerritos College
11110 East Alondra Boulevard
Norwalk, CA 90650

*City College of San Francisco
A.A. Legal Assisting Program
  and Legal Assisting
  Certificate Program I
50 Phelan Avenue
San Francisco, CA 94112

Coastline Community College
10231 Slater Avenue
Fountain Valley, CA 92708

Continental Technical Institute
Suite 410
9301 Wilshire Boulevard
Beverly Hills, CA 90211

Dominican College of San Rafael
San Rafael, CA 94901

Fresno City College
1101 East University Avenue
Fresno, CA 93741

Humphreys College
6650 Inglewood Drive
Stockton, CA 92507

Imperial Valley College
P.O. Box 158
Imperial, CA 92251

Lake Tahoe Community College
Legal Assistant Certificate
2659 Lake Tahoe Boulevard
P.O. Box 14445
S. Lake Tahoe, CA 95702

Los Angeles City College
855 North Vermont Avenue
Los Angeles, CA 90029

Los Angeles Southwest College
Legal Assistant Program
1600 West Imperial Highway
Los Angeles, CA 90047

Merritt College
12500 Campus Drive
Oakland, CA 94619

Orange Coast College
2701 Fairview Road
Costa Mesa, CA 92626

Pacific College of Legal Careers
Paralegal Studies Program
580 University Avenue
Sacramento, CA 95825

Pacific Legal Arts College
1387 Del Norte Road
Camarillo, CA 93010

Paralegal Training and Resource
  Center, Inc.
Suite 200
655 Sutter Street
San Francisco, CA 94102

Pasadena City College
Business Department
1570 East Colorado Boulevard
Pasadena, CA 91106

Pepperdine University
Legal Studies Program
8035 Vermont Avenue
Los Angeles, CA 90044

Rio Hondo College
Paralegal Program
3600 Workman Mill Road
Whittier, CA 90608

Rutledge College
5620 Kearney Mesa Road
San Diego, CA 92111

Sacramento City College
Dept. of Business and Social
  Science
3835 Freeport Boulevard
Sacramento, CA 95822

*St. Mary's College
Legal Assistant Certificate
Program A
P.O. Box 52
Moraga, CA 94575

San Bernardino Valley College
Legal Administration Program
701 South Mt. Vernon Avenue
San Bernardino, CA 92403

San Francisco State University
  Continuing Education/
  Extension
Paralegal Studies Program
1600 Holloway Avenue
San Francisco, CA 94132

San Joaquin College of Law
Paralegal Program
3385 East Shields
Fresno, CA 93726

Southeastern University
Legal Assistant Studies
San Jose, CA 95192

Santa Ana College
Seventeenth at Bristol
Santa Ana, CA 92706

Sawyer College of Business
6832 Van Nuys Boulevard
Van Nuys, CA 91405

Skyline College
Paralegal Program
3300 College Drive
San Bruno, CA 94066

Southland University
69 North Catalina
Pasadena, CA 91106

University of California at
    Irvine
Certificate Program in Legal
    Assistance
Irvine, CA 92717

*UCLA, University Extension
Attorney Assistant Training
    Program
10995 LeConte Avenue, Suite 214
Los Angeles, CA 90024

University of LaVerne
1950 Third Street
LaVerne, CA 91750

*University of San Diego
Lawyer's Assistant Program
Room 318, Serra Hall
Alcala Park
San Diego, CA 92110

University of Santa Clara
    Institute for Paralegal
    Education
Bannan Hall, Room 261
Santa Clara, CA 95053

*University of Southern
    California
Program for Legal
    Paraprofessionals
Law Center
University Park
Los Angeles, CA 90007

*University of West Los Angeles
School of Paralegal Studies
10811 Washington Boulevard
Culver City, CA 90230

West Valley College
1400 Fruitvale Avenue
Saratoga, CA 95070

Colorado

*Arapahoe Community College
Associate Degree Legal
    Assistant Program
5900 South Santa Fe Drive
Littleton, CO 80120

Colorado Paralegal Institute
609 West Littleton Boulevard
Suite 306
Littleton, CO 80120

Commuity College of Denver
Auraria Campus
Service Occupations Division
Room CA-313
1111 West Colfax
Denver, CO 80204

*Denver Paralegal Institute
General Practice Legal
    Assistant Program
Suite 908
1108 15th Street
Denver, CO 80202

Metropolitan State College
Legal Assistant Program
1006 11th Street
Denver, CO 80204

Pikes Peak Community College
5675 South Academy Boulevard
Box 19
Colorado Springs, CO 80906

Southern Colorado State College
Behavioral and Social Sciences
900 West Ormon
Pueblo, CO 81001

University of Denver
College of Law
Program of Advanced
    Professional Development
200 West 14th Avenue
Denver, CO 80204

Connecticut

Hartford College
Counseling Center for Women
1283 Asylum Avenue
Hartford, CT 06105

Institute for Legal Assistant
and Paralegal Training, Inc.
104 Bellevue Avenue
Bristol, CT 06010

Manchester Community College
Legal Assistant Program
P.O. Box 1046
Manchester, CT 06040

Mattatuck Community College
Legal Assistant Program
640 Chase Parkway
Waterbury, CT 06708

*Norwalk Community College
333 Wilson Avenue
Route 136
Norwalk, CT 06854

Post College
Legal Assistant Program
800 Country Club Road
Waterbury, CT 06708

*Quinnipiac College Legal
Studies Department
Mount Carmel Avenue
Hamden, CT 06518

*Sacred Heart University
P.O. Box 6460
Bridgeport, CT 06606

University of Bridgeport
600 University Avenue
Bridgeport, CT 06601

Delaware

Delaware Technical and
Community College
Southern Campus
Legal Assistant Technology
Georgetown, DE 19947

Goldey Beacom College
P.O. Box 5047
Wilmington, DE 19808

University of Delaware
Legal Assistant Education
Program
2800 Pennsylvania Avenue
Wilmington, DE 19806

Wesley College
Paralegal Program
Dover, DE 19901

District of Columbia

Antioch School of Law
Legal Technician Program
1624 Crescent Place, N.W.
Washington, DC 20009

*Georgetown University
School for Summer and
Continuing Education
Legal Assistant Program
Washington, DC 20057

*George Washington University
CEW Center—College of
General Studies
2130 H Street, N.W.
Library, Suite 621
Washington, DC 20052

Southeastern University
501 Eye Street, S.W.
Washington, DC 20024

University of the District of
Columbia
1331 H Street, N.W.
Washington, DC 20005

Florida

Barry College
11300 Northeast Second Avenue
Miami, FL 33161

Central Florida Commuity
  College
P.O. Box 1388
Ocala, FL 32670

Florida Atlantic University
Institute for Legal Assistants
Center for Management and
  Professional Development
Boca Raton, FL 33431

Hillsborough Community College
P.O. Box 22127
Tampa, FL 33622

Manatee Junior College
Legal Assistant Program
P.O. Box 1849
Bradenton, FL 33507

Miami Dade Community College
Legal Assistant Program
300 Northeast Second Avenue
Miami, FL 33312

Palm Beach Junior College,
  North
2101 45th Street
West Palm Beach, FL 33407

Pensacola Junior College
Legal Assistant Program
Pensacola Campus
1000 College Boulevard
Pensacola, FL 32504

St. Petersburg Junior College
Legal Assistant Program
Clearwater Campus
Coachman Road and Drew
Clearwater, FL 33515

St. Petersburg Junior College
Legal Assistant Program
P.O. Box 13489
St. Petersburg, FL 33733

*Santa Fe Community College
P.O. Box 1530
3000 Northwest 83rd Street
Gainesville, FL 32601

University of Central Florida
Allied Legal Services Program
P.O. Box 25000
Orlando, FL 32816

University of Miami
Institute for Paralegal Studies
P.O. Box 248005
Coral Gables, FL 33124

University of West Florida
Faculty of Political Science
Pensacola, FL 32504

Valencia Community College
East Campus
P.O. Box 3028
Orlando, FL 32802

Georgia

Gainesville Junior College
Legal Assistant Program
Mundy Mill Road
Gainesville, GA 30501

*National Center for Paralegal
  Training
Lawyer's Assistant Program
Suite 430
3376 Peachtree Road, N.E.
Atlanta, GA 30326

Hawaii

*Kapiolani Community College
Legal Assistant Program
620 Pensacola Street
Honolulu, HI 96814

Illinois

Illinois State University
Legal Studies Program
Department of Political Science
Schroeder 306
Normal, IL 61761

MacCormac Junior College
5825 Saint Charles Road
Berkeley, IL 60163

MacCormac Junior College
Room 420
327 South LaSalle Street
Chicago, IL 60604

*Mallinckrodt College
Legal Assistant Program
1041 Ridge Road
Wilmette, IL 60091

McKendree College
Paralegal Studies of
    Administration of Justice
College Road
Lebanon, IL 62254

Midstate College
Paralegal Services
244 S.W. Jefferson, Box 148
Peoria, IL 61602

National College of Education
Legal Assistant Program
2840 Sheridan Road
Evanston, IL 60201

The National Council of Black
    Lawyers
Community College of Law and
    International Diplomacy
Paralegal Studies
4545 South Drexel Boulevard
Chicago, IL 60653

*Roosevelt University
Lawyer's Assistant Program
430 South Michigan Avenue
Chicago, IL 60605

*Sangamon State University
Legal Studies Program
Shepherd Road
Springfield, IL 62708

*William Rainey Harper College
Legal Technology Program
Algonquin and Roselle Roads
Palatine, IL 60067

Indiana

Ball State University
Legal Assistance and
    Legal Administration
Muncie, IN 47306

Butler University
Legal Assistant Program
4600 Sunset
Indianapolis, IN 46208

Indiana Central University
1400 East Hanna Avenue
Indianapolis, IN 46227

*University of Evansville
Legal Paraprofessional
    Programs
P.O. Box 329
Evansville, IN 47702

Vincennes University
Paralegal Program
1002 North First Street
Vincennes, IN 47591

Iowa

Des Moines Area Community
2006 Ankeny Boulevard
Ankeny, IA 50021

*Kirkwood Community College
6301 Kirkwood Boulevard, S.W.
P.O. Box 2068
Cedar Rapids, IA 52406

Marycrest College
1607 West 12th Street
Davenport, IA 52804

Kansas

Barton County Community
    College
Legal Assisting
Great Bend, KS 67530

Hutchinson Community Junior
 College
Legal Assistant Program
1300 North Plum
Hutchinson, KS 67501

*Johnson County Community
 College
Paralegal Program
College Boulevard at Quivera
 Road
Overland Parks, KS 66210

*Wichita State University
Legal Assistant Program
College of Business
 Administration
Wichita, KS 67208

Kentucky

*Eastern Kentucky University
Legal Assistant Program
Lancaster Avenue
Richmond, KY 40475

Midway College
Paralegal Program
Midway, KY 40347

Sullivan Junior College
Institute for Paralegal Studies
3101 Bardstown Road
Louisville, KY 40205

Louisiana

Louisiana State University
 Law Center
Center of Continuing
 Professional Development
Room 275
Baton Rouge, LA 70803

Louisiana State University
8515 Youree Drive
Shreveport, LA 71115

Nicholls State University
Legal Assistant Studies
P.O. Box 2024, N.S.U.
Thibodaux, LA 70301

*Tulane University
University College
6823 Saint Charles Avenue
New Orleans, LA 70118

University of New Orleans
Legal Assistant Program
1001 Howard Avenue
New Orleans, LA 70113

Maine

Beal College
Paralegal Program
629 Main Street
Bangor, ME 04401

University of Southern Maine
Department of Conferences and
 Special Programs
96 Falmouth Street
Portland, ME 04103

Maryland

Community College of Baltimore
2901 Liberty Heights Avenue
Baltimore, MD 21215

Dundalk Community College
7200 Sollers Point Road
Baltimore, MD 21222

Harford Community College
Adult Occupational Education
401 Thomas Run Road
Bel Air, MD 21014

Para-Legal Institute
914 Silver Spring Avenue
Silver Spring, MD 20910

University of Maryland
University College
College Park Campus
College Park, MD 20742

*Villa Julie College
Legal Assistant Program
Greenspring Valley Road
Stevenson, MD 21153

Massachusetts

Anna Maria College
Paralegal Program
Paxton, MA 01612

Bay Path Junior College
Legal Assistant Program
588 Longmeadow Street
Longmeadow, MA 01106

Becker Jr. College
Paralegal Assistant
61 Sever Street
Worcester, MA 01609

*Bentley College
Institute of Paralegal Studies
Beaver and Forest Streets
Waltham, MA 02154

Boston State College
Paralegal Program
625 Huntington Avenue
Boston, MA 02115

Hampshire College
Amherst, MA 01002

Institute for Legal Assistant and
    Paralegal Training, Inc.
1193 Walnut Street
Newton Highlands, MA 02161

Middlesex Community College
Division of Continuing
    Education
Springs Road
Bedford, MA 01730

Mount Ida Junior College
Legal Assistant Program—
    Evening Division
777 Dedham Street
Newton Centre, MA 02159

Newbury Jr. College
Paralegal Program
921 Boylston Street
Boston, MA 02115

Northeastern University
Paralegal Program
7 Water Street
Boston, MA 02109

Regis College
Legal Studies Program
235 Wellesley Street
Weston, MA 02193

University of Massachusetts—
    Boston
Center for Legal Education
    Services
100 Arlington Street
Boston, MA 02116

Wentworth Institute of
    Technology
Legal Technology Program
40 Court Street
Boston, MA 02108

Michigan

Baker Junior College of Business
1110 Eldon Baker Drive
Flint, MI 48507

*Ferris State College
Legal Assistant Program
Big Rapids, MI 49307

Grand Valley State College
School of Public Service
College Landing
467 Mackinac Hall
Allendale, MI 49401

Henry Ford Community College
5101 Evergreen Road
Dearborn, MI 48125

Henry Ford Community College
22586 Ann Arbor Trail
Dearborn Heights, MI 48127

Hillsdale College
33 College Street
Hillsdale, MI 49242

Kellogg Community College
Legal Assistant Program
450 North Avenue
Battlecreek, MI 49016

Lansing Community College
Accounting and Office Programs
  Department
419 North Capitol Avenue
P.O. Box 40010
Lansing, MI 48901

Macomb County Community
  College
South Campus
14500 Twelve Mile Road
Warren, MI 48093

Madonna College
26600 Schoolcraft Road
Livonia, MI 48150

Mercy College of Detroit—
  Legal Assistant Program
Center for the Administration of
  Justice
8200 West Outer Drive
Detroit, Michigan 48219

Michigan Christian College
800 West Avon Road
Rochester, MI 48063

Michigan Paraprofessional
  Training Institute, Inc.
21700 Northwestern Highway
Suite 515
Southfield, MI 48075

Mott Community College
1401 East Court Street
Flint, MI 48503

Muskegon Business College
Paralegal Program
141 Hartford
Muskegon, MI 49442

*Oakland University
Diploma Program for Legal
  Assistants
Division of Continuing
  Education
Rochester, MI 48063

Minnesota

*Inver Hills Community College
Legal Assistant Program
8445 College Trail
Inver Grove Heights, MN 55075

*North Hennepin Community
  College
Legal Assistant Program
7411 85th Avenue North
Minneapolis, MN 55445

*University of Minnesota
General College
Legal Assistant Program
106 Nicholson Hall
Minneapolis, MN 55455

*Winona State University
Paralegal Program
4330 W-7
Winona, MN 55987

Mississippi

Mississippi University for
  Women
Paralegal Program
Department of Social Sciences
Columbus, MS 39701

Northwest Mississippi Junior
  College
Legal Assistant Program
300 North Panola Street
Senatobia, MS 38668

University of Mississippi
Paralegal Studies Program
Universities Center, Suite 116
Jackson, MS 39211

University of Southern
  Mississippi
Paralegal Studies
P.O. Box 5267, Southern Station
Hattiesburg, MS 39401

Missouri

*Avila College
11901 Wornall Road
Kansas City, MO 64145

Columbia College
Legal Assistant Program
Columbia, MO 64201

Maryville College
13550 Conway Road
St. Louis, MO 63110

Missouri Western State College
4525 Downs Drive
St. Joseph, MO 64507

Penn Valley Community College
Legal Technology Program
3201 S.W. Traffic Way
Kansas City, MO 64111

Rockhurst College
Evening Division
5225 Troost Avenue
Kansas City, MO 64110

St. Louis Community College
  at Florissant Valley
3400 Perhall Valley
St. Louis, MO 63135

St. Louis Community College
  at Forrest Park
5600 Oakland Avenue
St. Louis, MO 63110

St. Louis Community College
  at Meramec
11333 Big Bend
St. Louis, MO 63122

Southeast Missouri State
  University
Cape Girardeau, MO 63701

Webster College
470 East Lockwood
St. Louis, MO 63119

*William Woods College
Paralegal Studies Program
Fulton, MO 65251

Montana

College of Great Falls
Paralegal Education Program
1301 20th Street South
Great Falls, MT 59405

Nebraska

*Lincoln School of Commerce
Legal Studies Program
1821 K Street
P.O. Box 82826
Lincoln, NB 68501

Nevada

Reno Business College
Wells and Wonder
Reno, NV 89502

New Hampshire

McIntosh College
Legal Assistant Program
23 Cataract Avenue
Dover, NH 03820

*Rivier College
Baccalaureate and Certificate
  Paralegal Studies Programs
Nashua, NH 03060

University of New Hampshire
Paralegal Studies Program
Division of Continuing
  Education
Verrette House
6 Harrison Avenue
Durham, NH 03824

New Jersey

Bergen Community College
400 Paramus Road
Paramus, NJ 07652

Brookdale Community College
765 Newman Springs Road
Lincroft, NJ 07738

*Burlington County College
Pemberton–Browns Mills Road
Pemberton, NJ 08068

*Cumberland County College
Legal Technology Program
P.O. Box 517
Vineland, NJ. 08360

First School of Secretarial and
    Paralegal Studies
110 Main Avenue
Passaic Park, NJ 07055

First School of Secretarial and
    Paralegal Studies
516 Main Street
East Orange, NJ 07018

Institute for Legal Assistant
    and Paralegal Training
61 North Maple Avenue
Ridgewood, NJ 07450

Institute for Paralegal Studies
453 North Wood Avenue
Linden, NJ 07036

*Mercer County Community
    College
Legal Assistant Program
P.O. Box B
Trenton, NJ 08690

Middlesex County College
Legal Assistant Program
9 Ennis Drive
Hazlet, NJ 07730

*Montclair State College
Paralegal Studies Program
Upper Montclair, NJ 07043

Ocean County College
A.A.S. Legal Assistant
Toms River, NJ 08753

South Jersey Paralegal School
302 Sherry Way
Cherry Hill, NJ 08034

Sutton Paralegal School
1 Sutton Terrace
Collingswood, NJ 08107

Taylor Business Institute
250 Route 28
Post Office Box 6875
Bridgewater, NJ 08807

Upsala College
Paralegal Program
Office of Continuing Education
    Beck 205
East Orange, NJ 07019

New Mexico

Albuquerque Career Institute
2620 San Mateo Northeast
Albuquerque, NM 87110

Navajo Community College
Legal Advocates Training
    Program
P.O. Box 580
Shiprock, New Mexico 87420

University of Albuquerque
St. Joseph's Place, N.W.
Albuquerque, NM 87105

New York

*Adelphi University
University College
Division of Special Programs
Lawyer's Assistant Program
Garden City, NY 11530

Bronx Community College
University Avenue and West
    181st Street
Bronx, NY 10453

Broome Community College
Paralegal Assistant Program
P.O. Box 1017
Binghamton, NY 13902

Corning Community College
Paralegal Assistant Program
Spencer Hill Road
Corning, NY 14830

*Elizabeth Seton College
Legal Assistant Program
1061 North Broadway
Yonkers, NY 10701

Erie Community College
Main and Riley Streets
Buffalo, NY 14209

Herbert H. Lehman College
Legal Assistant Education
    Program
Bedford Park Boulevard
West Bronx, NY 10468

Herkimer County Community
    College
Herkimer, NY 13350

*Hilbert College
Legal Assistant Program
5200 South Park Avenue
Hamburg, NY 14075

Junior College of Albany
140 New Scotland Avenue
Albany, NY 12208

*Long Island University
Paralegal Studies Program
University Plaza
Brooklyn, NY 11201

Manhattanville College
Continuing Education
Purchase, NY 10577

Marist College
North Road
Poughkeepsie, NY 12601

Marymount Manhattan College
Continuing Legal Education
    Program
221 East 71st Street
New York, NY 10021

*Mercy College
White Plains Extension Center
Paralegal Studies Program
White Plains, NY 10601

Nassau Community College
Paralegal Assistant Program
Stewart Avenue
Garden City, NY 11530

*New York University
Institute of Paralegal Studies
School of Continuing Education
    in Law and Taxation
11 West 42nd St.
New York, NY 10036

Paralegal Institute
132 Nassau Street
New York, NY 10038

Queens College
Legal Assistant Program
65-30 Kissena Boulevard
Flushing, NY 11367

St. John's University
Legal Assistant Program
Grand Central and
    Utopia Parkway
Jamaica, Queens, NY 11439

Schenectady County Community
    College
Washington Avenue
Schenectady, NY 12305

Suffolk County Community
    College
A.A.S. Paralegal Studies
533 College Road
Selden, NY 11784

Sullivan County Community
    College
Paralegal Assistant Program
Lock Sheldrake, NY 12759

Syracuse University/University
    College
610 East Fayette Street
Syracuse, NY 13202

Westchester School for
  Paraprofessional Training
130 Ontario Street
Albany, NY 12206

Westchester School for
  Paraprofessional Training
275 Broadhollow Road
Melville, NY 11741

North Carolina

Central Carolina Technical
  Institute
Department of Community
  Colleges
1105 Kelly Drive
Sanford, NC 27330

Davidson City Community
  College
P.O. Box 1287
Intersection of Old Greensboro
  Road and Interstate 40
Lexington, NC 27292

*Fayetteville Technical Institute
P. O. Box 5236
Fayetteville, NC 28303

Greensboro College
Department of Business
  Administration, Legal
  Administration and Sociology
Greensboro, NC 27420

Meredith College
Legal Assistant Program
Department of Continuing
  Education
P.O. Box E-144
Raleigh, NC 27611

Pitt Technical Institute
Paralegal Program
P.O. Drawer 7007
Greenville, NC 27834

Southwestern Technical
  Institute
P.O. Box 95
Sylva, NC 28779

Ohio

Capital University
2199 East Main Street
Columbus, OH 43209

Clark Technical College
Box 570
Springfield, OH 45501

*Dyke College
Paralegal Education Programs
1375 East 6th Street
Cleveland, OH 44114

Hammel Actual College
59 East Market Street
Akron, OH 44308

Ohio Paralegal Institute
1001 Euclid Avenue
Suite 404
Cleveland, OH 44115

Paralegal Institute of the
  Western Reserve Academy of
  Paralegal Studies
Suite 201
Silver Building
Public Square
Wooster, OH 44691

Sinclair Community College
444 West Third Street
Dayton, OH 45402

University of Cincinnati
  Paralegal Program
University College, Mail
  Location #168
Cincinnati, OH 45221

*University of Toledo Paralegal
  Program
Scott Park Campus
2501 Bancroft
Toledo, OH 43606

Oklahoma

*Oscar Rose Junior College
Business Division
6420 Southeast 15th
Midwest City, OK 73110

Tulsa Junior College
Business Service Division
909 South Boston
Tulsa, OK 74119

*University of Oklahoma
C.L.E. Law Center
Paralegal Program
300 Timberdell, Room 314
Norman, OK 73019

Oregon

Clackamas Community College
Business Education Department
19600 South Molalla Avenue
Oregon City, OR 97045

Lane Community College
Business Department
4000 East 30th Avenue
Eugene, OR 97405

Mt. Hood Community College
26000 Southeast Stark Street
Gresham, OR 97030

Oregon State Department of
Education
942 Lancaster Drive, N.E.
Salem, OR 97310

*Portland Community College
Legal Assistant Program
Department of Government
Services
12000 Southwest 49th Avenue
Portland, OR 97219

Pennsylvania

Allegheny Community College
808 Ridge Avenue
Pittsburgh, PA 15212

*Cedar Crest College
Legal Assistant Program
Allentown, PA 18104

*Central Pennsylvania Business
School
College Hill Road
Summerdale, PA 17093

Community College of Allegheny
County
Boyce Campus
595 Beatty Road
Monroeville, PA 15146

Gannon College
Perry Square
Erie, PA 16501

Harrisburg Area Community
College
3300 Cameron Street Road
Harrisburg, PA 17110

Indiana University of
Pennsylvania Paralegal
Program
School of Business
Indiana, PA 15705

*The Institute for Paralegal
Training
235 South 17th Street
Philadelphia, PA 19103

King's College
Legal Assistant Program
Department of Criminal Justice
Wilkes Barre, PA 18711

Main Line Paralegal Institute
121 North Wayne Avenue
Wayne, PA 19087

Marywood College
Legal Assistant Program
Scranton, PA 18509

Misericordia College
Legal Assistant Program
Department of History and
Government
Dallas, PA 18612

Robert Morris College
Legal Assistant Certificate
Program
610 Fifth Avenue
Pittsburgh, PA 15219

Northampton County Area
   Community College
Legal Assistant Certificate
   Program
3835 Green Pond Road
Bethlehem, PA 18017

Pierce Junior College
1420 Pine Street
Philadelphia, PA 19102

Pennsylvania State University
Allentown Campus, Continuing
   Education
Academic Building
Fogelsville, PA 18051

Pennsylvania State University
Fayette Campus, Continuing
   Education
P.O. Box 519
Uniontown, PA 15401

The Pennsylvania State
   University
Paralegal Program
College of Business
   Administration
Continuing Education
403 Carpenter Building
University Park, PA 16802

Pennsylvania State University
McKeesport Campus, Continuing
   Education
University Drive
McKeesport, PA 15132

Pennsylvania State University
York Campus, Continuing
   Education
1031 Edgecomb Avenue
York, PA 17403

*Widener University
Delaware County
Chester, PA 19013

Puerto Rico

Universidad de Ponce
Legal Assistant Program
Avenida De Diego 700
Caparro Terrace, PR 00920

Universidad de Ponce
Legal Assistant Program
P.O. Box 648
Ponce, PR 00733

Rhode Island

Roger Williams College
Paralegal Studies
Old Ferry Road
Bristol, RI 02809

Salve Regina–The Newport
   College
Legal Assistant Program
Newport, RI 02840

South Carolina

Greenville Technical College
P.O. Box 5616 Station B
Greenville, SC 29606

*Midlands Technical College
P.O. Box 2408
Columbia, SC 29202

South Dakota

Yankton College
Legal Assistant Program
12th and Douglas
Yankton, SD 57078

Tennessee

*Cleveland State Community
   College
Legal Assistant Program
P.O. Box 3570
Cleveland, TN 37311

Memphis State University
Department of Business
   Administration
Memphis, TN 38152

University of Tennessee
Paralegal Training Program
Stokely Management Center
  (SMC) 608
Knoxville, TN 37916

Texas

Del Mar College
Legal Assistant Program
Baldwin and Ayers
Corpus Christi, TX 78404

East Texas State University
Department of Political Science
Commerce, TX 75428

El Centro College
Main and Lamar
Admissions Office
Dallas, TX 75202

El Paso Community College
Legal Assistant Program
El Paso, TX 79904

Grayson County College
Paralegal Program
Sherman, TX 75090

Houston Community College
  System
Legal Assistant Program
22 Waugh Drive
Houston, TX 77007

Lamar University
Continuing Education
P.O. Box 10008
Beaumont, TX 77710

St. Edwards University
Legal Assistant Program
Austin, TX 78704

San Antonio College
Legal Assistant Program
1300 San Pedro Avenue
San Antonio, TX 78284

Southwest Texas State
  University
Lawyer's Assistant Program
Mauldin House
San Marcos, TX 78666

*Southwestern Paralegal
  Institute
Basic Legal Assistant Studies
  Program
2411 Times Boulevard
Suite 27
Houston, TX 77005

Texas Institute for Paralegal
  Studies
Suite 102
1300 Guadalupe
Austin, TX 78701

Texas Para-Legal School—
  Houston
608 Fannin
Suite 1903
Houston, TX 77002

Texas Women's University
Department of History and
  Government
P.O. Box 23974
Denton, TX 76204

University of Houston at Clear
  Lake City
P.O. Box 20
Houston, TX 77058

University of Texas at Arlington
Paralegal Program
Department of Political Science
Arlington, TX 76019

West Texas State University
School of Business
Department of Business
  Education and Office
  Education
Canyon, TX 79016

Utah

Utah Technical College at Provo
Legal Assistant Program
Box 1009
Provo, UT 84601

Vermont

Champlain College
232 South Willard Street
Burlington, VT 05401

Virginia

Central Virginia Community
College
P.O. Box 584
Lynchburg, VA 24505

Elizabeth Brant School
Staunton, VA 24401

Ferrum College
Ferrum, VA 24088

James Madison University
Department of Political Science
Paralegal Studies Program
Harrisonburg, VA 22801

North Virginia Community
College
Alexandria Campus
3001 North Beauregard
Alexandria, VA 22311

Para-Legal Institute
Suite 300
6801 Whittier Avenue
McLean, VA 22101

J. Sargeant Reynolds
Community College
Parham Road Campus
P.O. Box 12084
Richmond, VA 23241

Thomas Nelson Community
College
Legal Assistant Program
P.O. Box 9407
Hampton, VA 23670

Tidewater Community College
Legal Assistant Program
1700 College Crescent
Virginia Beach, VA 23456

University of Richmond
University College Evening
School
Richmond, VA 23173

University of Virginia
104 Midmont Lane
Charlottesville, VA 22903

Virginia Western Community
College
3095 Colonial Avenue, S.W.
Roanoke, VA 24015

Washington

Bellevue Community College
Bellevue, WA 98007

Central Washington University
Program in Law and Justice
Ellensburg, WA 98926

City College
403–405 Lyon Building
Seattle, WA 98104

*Edmonds Community College
20000 68th Avenue West
Lynnwood, WA 98036

Fort Steilacoom Community
College
9401 Farwest Drive S.W.
Tacoma, WA 98498

*Highline Community College
Legal Assistant Program
Community College District 9
Midway, WA 98031

Lower Columbia College
Legal Assistant Program
1600 Maple
Longview, WA 98632

Spokane Community College
Legal Assistant Program
North 1810 Greene Street
Spokane, WA 99207

West Virginia

Fairmont State College
Legal Assistant Program
Division of Social Science
Fairmont, WV 26554

Marshall University
Community College
Legal Assistant Program
Huntington, WV 25701

Wisconsin

*Lakeshore Technical Institute
1290 North Avenue
Cleveland, WI 53015

Milwaukee Area Technical
  College
1015 North 6th Street
Milwaukee, WI 53203

District 1 Vocation Technical
  Adult Education
620 West Clairmont Avenue
Eau Claire, WI 54701

Appendix 2. Paralegal Associations in the United States

Many graduates of paralegal programs are interested in joining legal assistant associations. These associations perform both educational and social functions. As an organization interested in paralegalism as a career, a legal assistant association can provide seminars in continuing education for paralegals and a clearinghouse for employment opportunities for its members. It also serves as an educating body to inform attorneys how to utilize paralegals correctly and efficiently in the law office.

Socially, these legal assistant associations enable their members to form their own networking systems. If a paralegal member has a question concerning a legal procedure used by paralegals, he/she can contact another member of the organization for assistance. In addition, most associations have their own newsletters about developments in the paralegal field, individual members, as well as social events.

Most of these organizations require annual dues and hold monthly meetings. Membership dues are tax deductible.

The following is a list of legal assistant associations compiled by the American Bar Association.

Legal Assistant Associations

National Representative Associations

National Association of Legal Assistants, Inc.
Suite 122
3005 East Skelly Drive
Tulsa, OK 74105

National Federation of Paralegal Associations
Ben Franklin Station
P.O. Box 14103
Washington, D.C. 20044

Associations with Varied Membership

American Academy of Legal Assistants
Professional Arts Building
1022 Park Avenue, N.E.
Norton, VA 24273

American Paralegal Association
P.O. Box 35233
Los Angeles, CA 90035

State and Local Associations

(NALA) Denotes affiliation with National Association of Legal
Assistants

(NFPA) Denotes affiliation with National Federation of Paralegal Associations

Alaska

Alaska Legal Assistants Association
P.O. Box 1956
Anchorage, AK 99510

Arizona

Arizona Paralegal Association
P.O. Box 13083
Phoenix, AZ 85002

Tucson Association of Legal Assistants (NALA)
P.O. Box 257
Tucson, AZ 85702

California

East Bay Association of Legal Assistants (NFPA)
P.O. Box 424
Oakland, CA 94604

Los Angeles Paralegal Association (NFPA)
P.O. Box 24350
Los Angeles, CA 90024

Sacramento Association of Legal Assistants
P.O. Box 453
Sacramento, CA 95802

San Diego Association of Legal Assistants
P.O. Box 1649
San Diego, CA 92112

San Francisco Association of Legal Assistants (NFPA)
P.O. Box 26668
San Francisco, CA 94126

Colorado

Legal Assistants of Colorado (NALA)
c/o Mrs. Judy Poor, President
8432 Gray Court
Arvada, CO 80003

Rocky Mountain Legal Assistants Association (NFPA)
P.O. Box 304
Denver, CO 80210

Connecticut

Connecticut Paralegal Association
P.O. Box 134
Bridgeport, CT 06604

Delaware

Delaware Paralegal Association
P.O. Box 1362
Wilmington, DE 19899

District of Columbia

National Capital Area Paralegal Association (NFPA)
910 17th Street, N.W.
Suite 611
Washington, DC 20006

Florida

Florida Legal Assistants, Inc. (NALA)
c/o Ingrid Whigham
Director, Region VII
4221 Cherry Laurel Drive
Pensacola, FL 32504

Georgia

Atlanta Association of Legal Assistants
P.O. Box 1802
Atlanta, GA 30301

Georgia Association of Legal Assistants (NFPA)
P.O. Box 1802
Atlanta, GA 30301

Hawaii

Hawaii Association of Legal Assistants
P.O. Box 674
Honolulu, HI 96809

Illinois

Illinois Paralegal Association (NFPA)
P.O. Box 857
Chicago, IL 60690

Peoria Paralegal Association
c/o Paul G. Hammer
212 Johnson Street
East Peoria, IL 61611

Kansas

Kansas Legal Assistants Society
P.O. Box 774
Wichita, KS 67201

Kentucky

Louisville Association of Paralegals
P.O. Box 962
Louisville, KY 40201

Louisiana

New Orleans Paralegal Association
c/o Joyce E. Ludwig
305 Baronne Street
9th Floor
New Orleans, LA 70112

Maryland

Baltimore Association of Legal Assistants
c/o Lisa Dobbs
101 Linden Terrace
Towson, MD 21204

Massachusetts

Massachusetts Paralegal Association (NFPA)
P.O. Box 423
Boston, MA 02102

Michigan

Legal Assistants Association of Michigan (NALA)
c/o Florence M. Telling
2477 Bratton
Bloomfield Hills, MI 48013

Minnesota

Minnesota Association of Legal Assistants (NFPA)
P.O. Box 3712
Main Post Office
St. Paul, MN 55165

Missouri

Kansas City Association of Legal Assistants (NFPA)
P.O. Box 13223
Kansas City, MO 64199

Nebraska

Nebraska Association of Legal Assistants
P.O. Box 81434
Lincoln, NB 68501

New York

New York City Paralegal Association (NFPA)
FDR Station
P.O. Box 5143
New York, NY 10022

Ohio

Cleveland Association of Legal Assistants (NFPA)
P.O. Box 14011
Cleveland, OH 44114

Legal Assistants of Central Ohio
P.O. Box 15182
Columbus, OH 43215

Toledo Association of Legal Assistants (NALA)
201 Security Building
Toledo, OH 43604

Oregon

Oregon Legal Assistants Association
P.O. Box 8523
Portland, OR 97207

Pennsylvania

Pennsylvania Association of Legal Assistants (NALA)
c/o Janet Brown, President
1507 Robin Hill Apartments
Fourth and Preston Avenues
Voorhees, NJ 08043

Pennsylvania Paralegal Association
c/o Linda Malaney, President
Central Susquehanna Valley Legal Services
142 Market Street
Sunbury, PA 17801

Philadelphia Association of Paralegals (NFPA)
P.O. Box 55
Philadelphia, PA 19105

Pittsburgh Paralegal Association
P.O. Box 1053
Pittsburgh, PA 15230

Rhode Island

Rhode Island Paralegal Association
c/o Denise Aiken-Salandria
506 Industrial Bank Building
Providence, RI 02903

Texas

Dallas Association of Legal Assistants (NFPA)
P.O. Box 50812
Dallas, TX 75250

Virginia

Virginia Association of Paralegals
c/o Grace Robinson
McGuire, Woods and Battle
Ross Building
Richmond, VA 23219

Washington

Washington Legal Assistants Association (NFPA)
P.O. Box 2114
Seattle, WA 98111

Canada

Law Clerks of Ontario
347 Bay Street
Toronto, Canada

For further information about the paralegal profession, write to the American Bar Association at the following address:

Staff Director
ABA Standing Committee on Legal Assistants
1155 East 60th Street
Chicago, IL 60637

Index